Burn!
7 Leadership Myths in Ashes

Burn!
7 Leadership Myths in Ashes

Mitch McCrimmon

Published simultaneously in Canada and Great Britain in 2006 by
Self Renewal Group

171–110 Cumberland Street Second Floor
Toronto, Ontario   145–157 St John Street,
Canada M5R 3V5   London EC1V 4PY
                            United Kingdom

www.leadersdirect.com

Original paperback © 2006 by Mitch McCrimmon

All rights reserved. No part of this publication may be reproduced, stored in a retrieval system, or transmitted, in any form or by any means, electronic, mechanical, photocopying, recording or otherwise, without the prior permission of the publisher.

ISBN 0-9780080-0-6

Produced by Action Publishing Technology Ltd, Gloucester
Printed and bound in Canada

Contents

Introduction: Torching the 7 Myths of Leadership   1

Seven myths are torched to make room for *thought leadership*, the driving force of organizational renewal. Leadership is radically refocused on challenging the status quo to promote new directions, having *nothing to do with managing people or performance.*

PART ONE LEADERSHIP REBORN   13

1. The Leadership of the Outsider   15

Leadership from outsiders such as Martin Luther King or front-line knowledge workers challenges the status quo. Because they do not manage the people they lead, we finally have a clear way to separate leadership from management.

2. Management Reborn   30

Managers are not mechanical or controlling. They can empower, coach and inspire people to get things done. Management must be reborn to share the load with leadership.

3. The Sharp Edge of Leadership   46

Leadership focused on promoting new directions does not manage people. Because it simply challenges the status quo, it is based on the courage of convictions, youthful rebelliousness, not a learned skill set.

4. **What Executives Do If Not Lead**   63

   Executives are not leaders just by doing a good job but they can add value in other ways, especially by fostering leadership in others.

5. **The End of Primitive Leadership**   77

   Conventional leadership is paternalistic, based on the image of a protective parent. It is biologically primitive, thanks to our hard-wired habit of lining up in hierarchies. We must stop calling executives leaders. Leadership is an occasional act, not a role.

6. **Foster Leadership, Develop Executives**   89

   Leadership demands courage which isn't a learned skill. Like creativity it can only be fostered. "Leadership development programs" develop rounded executives, not leaders.

PART TWO   MORE MYTHS TO TORCH   107

7. **Kouzes and Posner on Leadership**   109

   This popular view of leadership is a confusing jumble of leadership and management notions because it originated in the 1980s when management was the scapegoat for the failure of the West to cope with the Japanese business invasion.

8. **Relationships: Women as Leaders**   119

   Are women better leaders than men because of relationship skills? But management, recast as a facilitative activity, requires stronger relationships than leadership. So, how is leadership a relationship?

9. **Character and Emotional Intelligence**   132

   Everyone in a responsible position needs to be trustworthy, even a lonely lighthouse operator, but leadership recast as challenging the status quo can be shown by people with poor interpersonal skills and zero emotional intelligence.

10. Leading, Influencing, Selling — 142

What is the relationship between leading and selling? What about teaching? What is the role of creativity? Teaching and selling are forms of influence, like leadership, but there are critical differences. Creativity overlaps with leadership, so you can be one, the other or both.

11. Organic or Mechanistic? — 149

The bandwagon to replace mechanistic with organic forms is the same as the move to replace managers with leaders, but businesses have two tasks: to get things done efficiently and create the future, so they need the best of both.

12. Servant Leadership — 160

This idea is plausible in clubs or associations where members have all the rights but not in business where the rights of owners (shareholders) trump those of employees.

13. Leadership with a Postmodern Twist — 165

Postmodernism torches authority, ushering in dispersed leadership. Severed from position, everyone is a leader who has something useful to say, just like in guerrilla warfare.

Notes and references — 179

Acknowledgements — 182

Index — 183

Introduction: Torching the 7 Myths of Leadership

Why is this book for you?

Are you an executive burdened by a grotesquely broad set of leadership expectations? Are you unsure whether to give direction, draw it out of others or just get out of the way? You're not alone. This book burns away the fog to sharpen your vision at work.

Are you a non-management employee with great ideas for new products or services? Do your bosses see themselves as the sole source of new ideas? Are you fed up waiting until you get promoted to show leadership? This book shows you how to lead NOW.

Does your business need to renew itself faster? Are you engaging and retaining employees as well as you could? Are they promoting new ideas as fervently as you want? In this book, you'll learn how thought leadership can get you where you're trying to go.

A revolution for leadership

Do you agree that everyone can show leadership today, that it isn't reserved for those in charge? But what does this mean? If it's nothing but the idea that anyone in a team can take charge informally, what is new? "Informal leadership" has been around for decades. Hyping it now is just rearranging the proverbial deck chairs. The same tired old model of leadership is firmly in place if being a leader still means taking charge of a group. A fresh start shows how leadership has nothing to do with managing anyone.

Why so radical? For these reasons:

- Complexity demands leadership from everyone.
- Innovation and continuous improvement are everyone's job.
- Bottom-up leaders advocate new directions. They don't take charge.
- Talent management demands full engagement.
- Leadership is now a guerrilla activity.
- Executives are creaking under too much ownership for results.

The truth is that conventional leadership theory is a bloated mess, but worse, it's the major obstacle to employee engagement and competitive advantage in the 21st century. A radically new beginning is long overdue. In this Introduction, I expose seven leadership myths to be consigned to the flames. Then I state what leadership really means, explain the benefits of the revolution and outline this book's chapters.

Seven leadership myths for burning

1. Leadership entails taking charge of people.
2. Leaders are transformational, managers transactional.
3. Leadership is a set of skills that anybody can develop.
4. Leaders require emotional intelligence and integrity.
5. Managers should be replaced by leaders.
6. Leadership entails working relationships with followers.
7. Great leaders soothe our anxieties.

The myths exposed

1. *Myth: Leadership entails taking charge of people.* The real meaning of leadership is to blast the status quo and advocate new directions, nothing else. How can leadership be shown bottom-up and from the sidelines, if it's about managing a team? Managers, not leaders, manage people. Leadership is not a role. But this doesn't mean that leadership means taking charge informally either. Leadership is not about taking charge at all.
2. *Myth: Leaders are transformational, managers transactional.* Leadership and management are functions, not styles or personality types. Function implies nothing about *how* to move people, so both can be transformational, inspiring, nurturing, caring and empowering. Also, leadership can be quiet, based on hard evidence cited with quiet conviction. It is total nonsense to define leadership so it rules out styles of influence that are not inspirational or transformational.
3. *Myth: Leadership is a set of skills that anybody can develop.* There are two requirements to show leadership – having something worth saying and the courage to say it. Being courageous enough to risk group rejection and ridicule stems from youthful rebelliousness. Courage is neither learned nor a skill. "Leadership development programs" spit out rounded executives, not leaders.
4. *Myth: Leadership demands emotional intelligence and integrity.* Anyone in a responsible position – managers, executives, even lighthouse operators – must be trustworthy. But leadership is like creativity in not being a role, hence not a type of responsibility. As a challenge to the status quo, it can be an aggressive and blunt guerrilla attack on authority from people with zero emotional intelligence as long as they make a strong case with hard evidence.
5. *Myth: Managers should be replaced by leaders.* This gross error dates from the 1980s Japanese onslaught that

exposed the West's poor competitiveness. Management was made the scapegoat for being bureaucratic and controlling. But who says it needs to be controlling? Leaders promote new directions. Managers get things done in a way that makes the best use of all resources and they can be as inspiring, supportive and empowering as they need to be. It is time to bring management back from the dead.
6. *Myth: Leadership implies a working relationship with followers.* Leadership can be shown at a distance, by outsiders, long dead leaders and even unintended example. In none of these cases is there a working relationship with followers. This matters because we turn potential leaders off by telling them they must beef up their relationship skills, or be quiet.
7. *Myth: Leaders soothe our anxieties.* This is the job of executives and managers. Leaders stir up trouble by calling for change and fuelling anxiety. Conventional leadership theory is riddled with paternalism. It is time to change how we view those in charge. We can lean on stronger people in tense times without calling them leaders. They are only substitute parents, doing what our mothers or fathers once did for us.

So, what?

Benefits of a radical remake of leadership theory

- Guerrilla leadership from all employees is critical for organizations to renew themselves faster. To fully engage employees at all levels, they need to see how they can show leadership now.
- Senior executives lack focus. Their role is bloated with two many expectations. Strategy entails focus; leadership slimmed down and management upgraded enables executives to add more value.

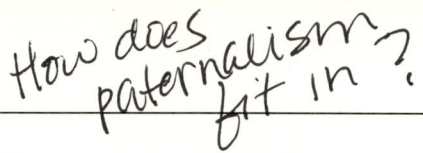
How does paternalism fit in?

- Empowerment has stalled. Employees wait for "leaders" to give direction. Explaining how all employees can show leadership takes empowerment to the next level, exorcizing dependency. This is *thought leadership*.
- We live in a world of innovation, a war of ideas. Thought leadership is the knowledge-age replacement for conventional positional leadership. Embrace it and win the next great lever of competitive advantage.
- Leadership is not a learnable skill but it doesn't matter because everyone can show leadership NOW. Every time you persuade someone to do something different, no matter how small the change, you show leadership. Buy this point and you can unleash all the leadership your organization can handle.

How to shift from the old to the new

What do these leadership idols have in common?

1. Martin Luther King
2. Gandhi
3. Nelson Mandela

Not their influencing style. King was an orator, Gandhi rather quiet. They had a vision, but here is what else:

- They attacked the status quo, providing new direction.
- The target audience was their respective governments.
- Crucially, they weren't in charge of the governments they led or even members of them. They didn't manage the people who implemented their visions, so their leadership was bottom-up or from the sidelines.

What emerges from the flames?

- Outsider leadership comes to an end once the target audience changes direction, so leadership can't be defined in terms of getting things done. Leaders sell the tickets for the journey. They do not drive the bus to the destination. This is management's job (the same person may or may not carry out both functions) King, Gandhi and Mandela were not in charge of their governments when they pushed for a new direction. Hence their leadership had nothing to do with managing those groups to implement the changes they championed.

- All notions of leadership based on how best to manage people who formally or informally report to a "leader" are wrong. So-called "leadership style" is really management style.
- Challenging the status quo can be aggressive and confrontational, as it was for King and Mandela, so leadership can't require relationship building skills or emotional intelligence.
- Founding leadership on what happens in groups paints a distorted picture because we focus on what it takes to become the head of a group and what the top person does in that role. We then point to personality or style differences, a total dead end, because many styles are possible. We must start over, and a good way of seeing this is to see how leadership is shown by people *who are totally outside their target groups*.

What is leadership?

Briefly, leadership is an occasional act, like creativity, not a role. You do not need to be creative to lead but you must champion something new. Some leaders have powerful influencing skills, but leadership isn't defined in terms of any influencing style just as our definition of creativity doesn't refer to selling skills. Leadership is an impact on a group that moves it to change direction. It can as easily come from outside the group or bottom-up as from the person in charge of the group.

> *Leadership does only one thing: it promotes a new direction.* It doesn't manage implementation or people. This is the radical twist, necessary to account for leadership from outsiders and bottom-up as well as the traditional top-down variety.

My argument for torching conventional leadership and starting afresh has the following steps:

PART ONE   LEADERSHIP REBORN

Part one is a sustained argument for a complete revision of leadership theory. Chapters are best read in order.

1. Chapter 1, *The Leadership of the Outsider*, shows that leadership must be recast as challenging the status quo to provide new directions. Whenever you challenge your boss and promote novel ideas for new products or better ways of doing things, you show thought leadership. Like the outsider leadership of Martin Luther King, Gandhi and Nelson Mandela, such leadership comes to an end once your boss buys your ideas. Management might implement your idea or delegate it to someone other than you. You might have poor management skills or not be interested in managing a team. I explain how thought leadership can be shown by all employees with the courage to promote good ideas to their bosses. This is bottom-up leadership.
2. Chapter 2, *Management Reborn*, brings management back from the dead as a supportive, empowering, facilitative and inspiring function to take the lion's share of moving people from A to B. Conventional leadership theory is fossilized because it is stuck on how people in charge get things done. This leads to the tired old binary oppositions of consideration for people versus providing structure, theory Y versus theory X, demo-

cratic versus autocratic, transformational versus transactional. Mysteriously, leadership got associated with the good guy side of these pairs (consideration for people, theory Y, etc.) while management was consigned to the bad guy role. This is a gross error because style questions arise only when we focus on persons in roles instead of functions: leadership to promote new directions and management to implement them. The *means or style* of moving people is a separate question. Hence, managers can be as transformational, empowering and considerate as leaders. The bottom line is that 80 percent of what executives do is management, not leadership.

3. Chapter 3, *The Sharp Edge of Leadership,* shows that leadership equals having something worthwhile to say plus the courage to say it. Leadership strictly focused on challenging the status quo can be displayed across the spectrum of influencing styles from quiet and matter-of-fact through a blunt confrontation to an uplifting, emotionally engaging vision. But, because leadership has nothing to do with managing people, the nature of leadership is much sharper. Out of the fog we now see that courage is the number one personal trait underpinning leadership which, like creativity, isn't a learnable skill. Only influencing skills can be learned. This chapter burns off many popular leadership myths.

4. Chapter 4, *What Executives Do When Not Leading,* explores how executives add value when not leading. If being effective in your role doesn't automatically make you a leader, how else can you contribute? If leadership isn't arc-welded to position, what do executives do? The answer: leadership is only one of several functions that executives perform. A surprising result is that executives show leadership only when change is needed. They run successful businesses without showing much leadership.

5. Chapter 5, *The End of Primitive Leadership,* addresses a

highly emotive subject. What is the status of the traditional leader, the person we look up to for strength in times of crisis to soothe our anxieties and help us reduce uncertainty? This notion of leadership is hopelessly paternalistic because such leaders are substitute father figures. It is also biologically primitive because all higher animals are hard-wired to form into hierarchies. We need to relabel people in charge as executives even if we can't avoid wanting someone strong to lean on or stop living in hierarchies. We will fail to develop a concept of leadership in tune with our need for rampant innovation unless we dump this outworn image.

6. Chapter 6, Foster *Leadership, Develop Executives,* attacks the conventional wisdom that leadership can be developed. I argue that influencing skills can be learned, as can finding something worth saying, but the courage to speak up is not acquired in a classroom or from experience. Like creativity, leadership can only be fostered, not developed. Programs that claim to develop leaders give us rounded executives, not leaders.

PART TWO   MORE MYTHS TO TORCH

Part Two covers issues in more depth that were left out of Part One to make it a faster read. Each chapter in Part Two stands alone and can be read in any order.

7. Chapter 7, *Kouzes and Posner on Leadership,* discusses the popular book, *The Leadership Challenge.*[1] There is no place for management in Kouzes and Posner's world because they started writing in the 1980s when management was the scapegoat for U.S. industry's failure to cope with the Japanese onslaught. One of Kouzes and Posner's principles captures the essence of leadership, "challenge the process," but they dilute it

to plain water by saying that leaders only stimulate others to challenge the process. Leaders are facilitators for them, what I see as managers. Leadership is at its most bloated in *The Leadership Challenge*.

8. Chapter 8, *Relationships: Women as Leaders*, explodes the truism that you can't be a leader without followers. This innocent idea is mistakenly taken to imply actual working relationships between people. I argue that leadership can be shown at a distance and by long dead leaders; hence there need not be actual working relationships between leaders and followers. Also, people can challenge the status quo aggressively with poor relationship skills. This undermines the claim that women might be better leaders than men by having stronger relationship skills. They might be good managers though, because management does require excellent relationship skills. Now we can explain how people without relationship skills can show leadership in a quiet, factual or obnoxious manner.

9. Chapter 9, *Character and Emotional Intelligence*, argues that such traits are certainly critical for anyone in responsible *positions*. Even a lighthouse operator needs to be trustworthy. But leadership is never a role or position. Having the skills of diplomacy and sensitivity makes you a better influencer, but this is a situational requirement, not a necessary condition, because leadership can be an aggressive, confrontation based on hard facts. The bottom line is that character and emotional intelligence are essential for the rounded executive or manager but not for leadership.

10. Chapter 10, *Leading, selling, teaching and creating*, looks at the relationship between these factors and the place of creativity. Do leaders teach or sell? What forms of influence count as leadership? Must you be creative or innovative to lead and, if not, what is the place of these elements in leadership? This chapter presents a fine-grained picture of how leadership works by

comparing it with factors that are often confused with it.
11. Chapter 11, *Organic or Mechanistic?* is important because the drive to replace mechanistic structures with the organic precisely parallels the push to replace management with leadership for many of the same reasons. I argue that all organizations need to be a mixture of both organic and mechanistic elements. Leadership is organic because it emerges spontaneously from the front-lines or anywhere else inside or outside the organization while management is mechanistic, not in the sense of robotic or mechanical, but by being a role that emphasizes deliberate planned action and consistent output, essential for cost control, uniform quality and predictable service levels.
12. Chapter 12, *Servant Leadership,* shows this to be a confused notion, applicable only in clubs, associations or politics where the person in charge is specifically there to serve group members. Business serves customers and shareholders whose needs can't be sacrificed to employee needs. At best, it might be sensible to talk of servant management, but leadership can upset employees by challenging the status quo. Leaders generate better offerings for customers, not serve employees.
13. Chapter 13, *Leadership With a Postmodern Twist,* paints the big picture to show how leadership radically transformed fits with broader trends, specifically postmodernism, the idea that there is no universal authority on anything. I sever leadership from the authority of position. Good ideas can't be monopolized by one person, unlike a slot in a hierarchy. Everyone can show some leadership by promoting something new. Hence we're all our own authorities. I show how our quest to understand leadership over the past century has failed because of our focus on the *dynamics within groups*. In a postmodern world, group boundaries fragment. We need a vision of leadership that crosses traditional group lines.

This book covers a lot of ground in a short space. I have aimed to make it as easy to digest as possible by keeping the chapters short and to the point. Dividing it into two quite separate parts also helps. Part One sets out my core argument with a minimum of complexity and digression into side issues. Part Two picks up some of the many leadership topics that are left out of Part One.

Part One
LEADERSHIP REBORN

PART ONE is a sustained argument for a completely new model of leadership. As the core of the book, its chapters are best read in order.

The first step is to carve out a form of leadership that has nothing to do with management. We gain a much clearer distinction between leadership and management than any available today. To limit leadership to promoting new directions, I upgrade management to carry the load of getting everything done through people. This is achieved by sketching a much more empowering, supportive and inspiring concept of management. Focusing leadership on challenging the status quo places the courage of one's convictions at the heart of leadership implying that it isn't a wholly learnable skill set. The bottom line is that leadership, like creativity, can only be fostered. Rounded executives and managers are developed by "leadership development programs."

A crucial step is my argument is showing that we need to exorcize the paternalistic image of leadership from our minds. We may not shake off our need to rely on those in positions of authority to look after us but we can stop calling them leaders. Without this step, we'll fail to reap the rewards of thought leadership, so essential for competitive advantage in our knowledge-driven age.

Part Two, *More Myths To Torch*, covers critical implications of my reformulation of leadership for a range of issues in conventional leadership theory but its chapters do not need to be read in order. You might read only those that particularly interest you.

CHAPTER 1

The Leadership of the Outsider

LEADERSHIP AND MANAGEMENT are either lumped together in a confused mess or poorly separated. We go around in circles on this issue because we persist in starting with how one person in charge of a group both leads and manages.

To see how leadership differs from management, consider examples where the leader has nothing to do with managing people or implementation. Bottom-up and outsider leadership finally give us a wedge to drive leadership and management apart with striking clarity.

Examples of non-positional leadership

- Martin Luther King, Gandhi and Nelson Mandela were outsiders when they showed leadership to their respective governments.
- Bottom-up thought leaders influence senior executives without being members of the executive team.
- Ground-breaking companies lead competitors: Apple with iTunes, Google and Netscape, have led Microsoft.
- Industry gurus show leadership to knowledge workers in several organizations.

How often have you pushed an idea in a meeting that changed your colleagues' thinking? Your leadership did not amount to chairing the discussion. Instead, you made a unique contribution to the *content* of the debate. This is thought leadership. Whenever you influence a team of which you're not a member, you lead from the outside. This is counterintuitive because leadership is usually portrayed as shown exclusively by group members informally to each other or formally by the head of a group.

Outsider leadership: King, Gandhi and Mandela

When Martin Luther King organized a boycott of buses to protest against segregation in Montgomery, Alabama, he showed leadership to the City of Montgomery, the state of Alabama and the U.S. government. His leadership succeeded when the U.S. Supreme Court declared bus segregation unconstitutional. He led several protest marches in his career. His followers in the streets, however, could be seen as joining him on the leadership stage in his challenge to the status quo by creating a stronger impact on those in power, thereby showing leadership too.

This turns the usual picture on its head as King's target followers were the people in government he wanted to influence, while his street followers actually showed leadership alongside him. Not being a member of any of his target governments, let alone in charge of them, King's leadership was that of an outsider, an instance of bottom-up leadership. *His leadership came to an end once his target audience bought and implemented his vision. Execution was a separate phase that did not involve him.*

Gandhi championed the cause of Indian independence from British rule through mass strikes and protests. He advocated non-violent civil disobedience to challenge the rule of Britain over India. Although he was imprisoned a number of times over several years, the British finally granted Indian independence in 1944. Again, relative to the British government, the group he was trying to influence, Gandhi was an outsider, neither a member nor in charge of his target follower group. Like Martin Luther King, his leadership was directed upward at those who had formal authority over his country.

Nelson Mandela's ANC movement started protesting against apartheid and white minority rule in South Africa on a non-violent basis which later unfortunately degenerated into violence. Like Gandhi and King, Mandela spent time in prison but he was ultimately successful in bringing white majority rule to an end. Like King and Gandhi, Mandela was an outsider relative to the group in power that he sought to influence.

Do these examples merely illustrate "informal" leadership? No, because informal leadership refers to *taking charge* to get things done informally within groups of which the informal leaders are members. Outsider leadership is directed upward at the source of authority where the person leading isn't a member of that group. This is a completely new model of leadership.

Note that none of these leaders could implement their visions by working *through* their followers on the street. They could only influence those in power, hoping that they would buy the message and act on it.

> The point here is both obvious and revolutionary. The crux of my whole argument is that outsider leaders do not manage the people who implement their visions. Hence leadership can't be defined in terms of getting things done through a team. It must therefore be simply challenging the status quo to provide new directions.

Thought leadership

Thought leadership is the critical form of leadership in knowledge-driven organizations, the successor to positional leadership necessary for prosperity wherever innovation is critical to success. It is shown by employees who are not *in charge* of the people they show leadership to, even informally. It is the upward promotion of ideas for new products, services or processes. Like the leadership of King, Gandhi and Mandela, thought leaders have no formal authority over anyone, let alone their bosses. They are front-line knowledge workers leading senior executives by challenging the status quo.

Gary Hamel advocates bottom-up thought leadership in *Leading the Revolution,* but he doesn't call it that. As he explains, "Activists are changing the shape of companies around the world. At Sony, a midlevel engineer challenges top management to overcome its prejudice against the video game business. 'We do not make toys!' they protest. He badgers, plots and schemes. Against all odds he persuades Sony to develop the PlayStation."[1] Hamel doesn't develop a supporting model of leadership despite calling for it, which shows what a strong hold the conventional model of leadership has on us.

Examples of thought leadership

Ask yourself which of these examples exhibit leadership and how? What do you learn about leadership from them?

1. Jane[2] is a new help desk associate recruited from a market leading competitor. Her excellent training enables her to serve her new users so well that everyone asks for her. Jane isn't aware that she is leading her colleagues to follow her example.
2. Phillip, a young accountant, pushes for more transparency in his employer's financial reporting. He isn't inspiring, but his boss is convinced by the evidence Phillip cites.
3. Carlos is a lone software developer working at home on spam blocking software. His new technique is quickly copied by other developers around the world.
4. A team of auto assemblers meets to brainstorm ways to improve quality. Jim sees a better way to organize one of their steps that would significantly reduce errors, something he would never have thought of without this brainstorming meeting. Jim isn't seen as a leader by any of his colleagues but his idea is so good,

he has little trouble convincing the others.
5. Wendy, a junior doctor, listens to senior colleagues advocating a new surgical procedure. Wendy then quietly cites hard evidence for the superiority of the current procedure and persuades her colleagues that more research is needed before adopting the new one.
6. Sarah, an HR Director, convinces the regional heads to adopt a new performance appraisal system. She has no authority to force compliance and doesn't manage her colleagues but they finally come around. Sarah doesn't manage implementation.
7. Peter is a junior product developer in a consumer electronics company who is very creative but not much liked because he attacks the ideas of his colleagues aggressively. But Peter is valued for his stunning ideas for new products and, for this reason, often wins his colleagues over.

Leadership lessons in these examples

1. Jane influenced her colleagues on the help desk without even realizing it, proving that leadership doesn't require inspirational influencing skills. Leadership is too often portrayed as a deliberate attempt to persuade a group to undertake a task it would not otherwise do. But we know intuitively that a great deal of leadership is actually shown by example. Why do we conveniently ignore this fact? Leadership by example can be shown upward and sideways as well as down while leadership-as-team-management is downward by definition, a very narrow view of leadership.
2. Phillip's advocacy of more transparency in Finance was logical and factual, hence little more inspirational than Jane's. Because Phillip had no authority to change the process on his own, his leadership came to an end once his manager bought his idea. Implementation was

managed by Phillip's boss. Hence, leadership doesn't require the leader to be involved in getting things done, unlike the person in charge of the group who we would normally see as the real leader. Here, implementation was a management undertaking. The leadership was over and done before implementation took place.

3. Carlos, the innovative software developer, isn't very persuasive, being a quiet person, but no problem because his followers were opportunists. Hence the need to be inspirational depends on the amount of resistance the leader faces rather than being the essence of leadership. We admire those who overcome massive resistance more than leaders whose followers are opportunists, but this says more about our need for heroes than it does about leadership. Also, none of Carlos's "followers" knew him, let alone worked with him. Mainstream leadership theory ignores this fact by characterizing leadership as an activity that occurs only within groups where there's a working relationship between leader and followers.

4. Jim had no idea how to improve their assembly process until the team started brainstorming. His leadership stems from the stimulation of his colleagues rather than any special qualities he brought to the party. Such leadership is *emergent*, like spontaneous combustion, an activity that can occur anywhere outside of formal roles. But being thus contextual doesn't mean it's limited to actual working teams.

5. Wendy's defence of the existing surgical procedure shows that action isn't always an outcome of leadership. It's only confused with getting things done when we focus erroneously on the person in charge of the group who might well both lead and manage implementation.

6. Sarah, the HR Director, showed leadership to her peers when she promoted a new performance appraisal system. Having no power to force compliance, she cited hard evidence passionately, so being inspira-

tional helped. But, as in the other examples, Sarah's leadership is a separate phase from managing the implementation. That was done by her colleagues who did not report to Sarah.
7. Peter, the aggressive product developer succeeds in showing leadership to his team and to his bosses solely because he offers convincing evidence for the viability of his ideas. He shows leadership *in spite of* having zero emotional intelligence.

Another example

John Wells, a product developer in an electronics company, convinced senior management to abandon their best selling product for something completely new.

> I asked John "How did you convince management to ditch your most profitable product?'
>
> 'I initially tried a softly, softly approach, one to one with key senior people. They wouldn't listen. Then I got mad. I wangled a chance to address the Board about a new product my team was developing. They expected a polite, deferential presentation, so they were shocked when I hit them between the eyes with both barrels.'
>
> "Sounds exciting!" I replied. "What did you actually say to them?"
>
> "I told them they were a bunch of idiots if they couldn't see the writing on the wall, that their pet product was going down the tubes if they didn't wake up and see what our competitors were doing. I cursed and swore, ranted and raved. They sat in stunned silence."
>
> "And then what happened, John?"
>
> "All hell broke loose. A couple of them really lost it, but the Chief executive shushed them up and asked me some sensible questions. The next day I was told they were taking my advice."
>
> "What do you think made your leadership work?"

"I just got really passionate about what we were doing. It didn't matter that I upset a few people; I woke them up and swung the group. I had to have the guts to speak up forcefully and paint a dire picture, but I figured I had nothing to lose so I went for it. I'm glad I did and I've got a lot more respect around here as a result."

John's leadership was bottom-up. He didn't manage anyone, certainly not the executive team, and he wasn't asked to manage the new product once it was launched.

Business gurus as thought leaders

Seth Godin's *Permission Marketing*[3] challenges what he calls "interruption marketing", advertisements thrust in our faces everywhere we look. Godin advocates permission marketing to niche markets where consumers volunteer to receive marketing messages. Godin's thought leadership could have a huge impact on companies that spend millions on advertising, yet he isn't an employee or manager in any such companies. This is pure leadership because it induces people (marketing departments in large companies) to do things they might not have done and without Godin's involvement in making anything happen.

Tom Peters has been a thought leader for years, promoting new ways to unleash the full energies and talents of employees. His ideas have had a leadership impact on businesses that adopted his proposals.

Burning implications of these examples

In *The Leadership Challenge* Kouzes and Posner tell us "In this book, and in all our discussions of leadership, we use the journey metaphor to express our understanding of leadership."[4] People in charge of groups surely oversee whole journeys but there is a chasm between leadership and the implementation journey in the examples above.

> Leadership sells the tickets for the journey; it doesn't drive the bus to the destination.

People in charge switch hats from leader to manager after selling the need to act. Enroute, the benefits of the journey might need to be resold by an injection of leadership if the travellers are no longer keen on the journey. Otherwise only good management skills, recast in a facilitative light, are required to get to the destination.

Because John Wells and Peter, the software developer, promote new products aggressively, they must rely on hard evidence to make their cases. Peter's colleagues do not trust him, thanks to his low emotional intelligence. But they buy his ideas because he demonstrates their value. What matters is the quality of his ideas, not who he is or what he is like as a person. Peter isn't able to manage the team at this stage in his career and no one would want his advice on how to work more effectively. Much is written by Daniel Goleman and others about the importance of emotional intelligence, character or integrity for leaders. Such qualities are essential for managers, but leadership is about challenging the status quo, aggressively or otherwise.

Influencing style can range from an abrasive sales pitch delivered by an obnoxious eccentric with zero emotional intelligence to very emotionally intelligent, visionary or diplomatic overtures. For leadership, emotional intelligence is just a situational influencing style, not its essence.

Here are the main features of thought leadership:

- It is an occasional act that influences what a group thinks, believes or values, not a role, formal or informal.
- It has nothing to do with organizing, directing or coordinating the work of others to get a task done, hence nothing to do with managing, coaching, developing or empowering people.

- It is egalitarian. No one can monopolize good ideas unlike a position in a hierarchy.
- It can range from revolutionary new business concepts to slight modifications in the way work is done, which means that everyone can show some thought leadership, even if only at the incremental end of the scale.
- It can be shown up, sideways and down.
- It comes to an end the moment the new ideas are accepted. Implementation is a separate phase that may or may not be undertaken by the same person. It changes what people think and doesn't necessarily result in any action.
- Much thought leadership is based on innovation, but it need not be. Championing transparency in accounting practices, for example, is based on age-old ethical principles, not innovation.
- It consists in promoting ideas for change, challenging the status quo. It isn't a matter of *facilitating* new thinking in others, but of actually making a substantive contribution to the content of a conversation.
- It can be shown by example or by obnoxious guerrilla attacks. All that matters is that followers buy the ideas. Some followers are such opportunists that they don't care how the message is delivered. Others are moved only by irrefutable evidence, some by an emotional hook. None of these forms of influence is common to all leadership, so none is definitional for leadership.
- It depends on technical, not personal, credibility, integrity, emotional intelligence or values. The citing of values is a specific influencing tactic that is only required when the aim is to get people aligned to certain values. What we might call *values leadership* doesn't apply in technical areas.
- It can be shown at a distance, as when technical people follow the lead of an industry guru, so it isn't based on relationships within working teams. Relationships are clearly vital for managers to get things done, but they are only situational influencing tactics for leading

people. Martin Luther King's leadership is still felt by people today, long after his death, so leadership can't require close working relationships or be confined to teams of people that actually work together.

How can you show leadership?

What new initiatives can you promote?

Can you think of a new product or service (content leadership), new process such as improved customer service, quality or cost reduction (process leadership) that you can champion? You don't have to be personally innovative. You might find something worth standing up for by brainstorming or networking with others.

How comfortable are you to challenge the status quo? If you're not sure, start small. Advocate small changes and do so with diplomacy and emotional intelligence. You might even make your target audience think it was their idea. See the box below.

	2 High personal risk, low payoff, getting angry over small things	**3** High personal risk, high payoff. Passion on the line for large stakes, most courageous leadership
Aggressive, blunt influencing style		
Emotionally intelligent, diplomatic style	**1** Lowest risk leadership initiative, everyday acts of leadership	**4** Low personal risk, could be visionary and inspiring, but high payoff.
	New ideas for minor changes	New ideas for radical changes

Box 1: This is the place to be if you're not accustomed to raising your head above the parapet. Thousands of instances of such low risk leadership initiatives occur every day in all organizations. Here you're promoting a minor change in a product or operational process.

Box 2: This is the worst place to be. Throwing a temper tantrum for little return isn't clever.

Box 3: You might never want to be here either. While the potential return is greater, you're sticking your neck out in two ways – white hot emotional expression combined with a radical idea. Two chances to get shot down, ridiculed, laughed at, rejected. But sometimes such strong leadership needs to be shown by someone, especially when you're trying to lead upwards and you're attacking deeply entrenched views. This was how John Wells showed what he was made of.

Box 4: This is a nice place to be. Your style will not ruffle any feathers so the only risk you're taking is by promoting such an outlandish idea. But sometimes a vision conveyed with enthusiasm, warmth and sensitivity isn't enough to move the powers that be.

The only thing common to all four boxes is the promotion of something new. This is the core of leadership. Your style needs to flex in line with the resistance of your target audience, a situational requirement, nothing to do with the meaning of leadership. This must be true if a hard-hitting, aggressive style can be as effective in some circumstances as a warmer, more diplomatic one.

Can't think of anything worth getting excited about?

To show leadership, you must have something new to say. But you don't have to rely on navel gazing, thinking in isolation, to come up with something worth sticking your neck out for. The development of good ideas is interactive. It is critical to network and brainstorm actively with a select group of internal and external leading edge people who might have an inside track. This is the best way to discover something worth getting sufficiently worked up about to show leadership.

Benefits of thought leadership

- Organizations are better able to motivate knowledge workers to champion new ideas by labelling them leadership acts.
- Employees are more engaged in determining the direction of their employer rather than depending on top down leadership.
- A better division of leadership effort creates broader ownership and commitment, freeing executives to focus on issues where they can add most value.
- Executives acquire stronger facilitative, nurturing and listening skills to encourage leadership in all employees. This no longer means preparing them for promotion but rather stimulating them to show leadership now.
- An examination of outsider or bottom-up leadership sheds invaluable light on the fundamental nature of all leadership. It also finally gives us the key to differentiate leadership from management.

To foster upward leadership in your team

- Be less self-reliant in deciding direction.
- Draw out more ideas with good questions.
- Get people to practice making sales pitches to you.
- Celebrate and reward those who take a stand.
- Avoid being defensive when challenged.

Tom Bower's questions and my replies

Tom Bower, a successful construction company executive, asked me

> "Why should we buy your idea that leadership should be limited to challenging the status quo and providing new directions?"

I replied "Because it's the only way to account for non-positional leadership where the person showing it isn't in charge of anyone and who has no interest in managing a team."

"But why has no one else come up with this angle before?"

"Because we're locked onto the person in charge of the group as our paradigm case of leadership. We're hard-wired to fall into place in a hierarchy. Hence we want to know what it takes to rise to the top and hold such a powerful position over people."

"So what's wrong with that?"

"Leadership in our knowledge-driven age is about promoting new ideas, not gaining power over people. By modelling leadership on taking charge of groups to get things done, we overlook a powerful motor of innovation and continuous improvement. We need to take empowerment to the next stage so everyone can show leadership without having to manage the implementation of their ideas."

"Are you saying that leadership is nothing but advocating good ideas. Surely, that's not enough if nothing gets done."

"I agree that no leadership occurs if people don't act on the new ideas or accept them, so merely promoting new ideas is not enough. My point is that it's *possible* to show leadership merely by influencing people to buy ideas without the leader being involved in implementing them. Using the 80-20 rule, it's likely that most people who promote doing something different also take part in making it happen. But when they switch to implementation mode, they put on a manager's hat – which I explain in the next chapter. If you grant me that, at least sometimes, leadership stops at promoting new directions, that's enough to force us to define leadership so that it doesn't entail taking charge of getting things done. Just because I define leadership as successfully influencing people to buy a new direction, I'm not committed to the absurd view that people who show leadership never get involved in implementing that direction."

Tom wasn't convinced yet as I hadn't explained how to rehabilitate management to fill the gap he was sensing in the vital arena of getting things done. This is the subject of the next chapter.

CHAPTER 2

Management Reborn

IT IS TIME to bring management back from the dead to be enabling, supportive and empowering, not controlling.

What is management?

Recall John Wells sticking his neck out to champion a new product and who won the day because of his evident passion and the strong business case he presented to senior management. When he was promoted to a manufacturing management role, I asked him:

"So, John, do you see yourself as a leader now?"

John replied "I showed some leadership when I championed our new product, but now I'm mainly a manager. I need to execute, to make this product cost-effectively and at the required level of quality. This means getting the best out of everyone on my team. I see that as being a good manager."

"And what makes a good manager in your opinion, John?"

"I see it as a combination of task and people skills. On the task side, I make sure the numbers stack up and that everyone is doing the right things. On the people side, I need to inspire employees to work hard, to think for themselves and to make good decisions. This means being a good facilitator, listener, coach and nurturer."

"And how do you think you're doing?"

"Too soon to tell. Instinctively, I'm a bit of a troublemaker. I like to stir things up, which I see as a core leadership attribute. I've got a lot of learning to do before I can call myself an effective manager."

Notice that John slightly evaded my first question. I asked him if he was *a* leader, but he said he *showed some* leadership but was *a* manager. This is correct. Leadership is an occasional act while management is a role. You can *be* a manager but you can only *show* leadership. Also, note that John sees the need, as a manager, to *both* initiate structure *and* show consideration for people, to do the right things *and* things right. These time-worn mantras, therefore, do not serve as a basis to differentiate leadership from management, as so many think.

The manager as coach

In team sports the coach is sometimes called the manager. This image, the manager-as-coach, is what we need, not that of a mechanistic controller or overseer.

The controlling manager is a machine operator with employees as properly working or faulty machine parts. This was how Frederick Taylor viewed management in assembly-line days. By contrast, sports managers have no direct control over what happens on the playing field. The game evolves on its own with only the players able to influence the outcome. The sports manager can coach and develop players, select and fire them, but can't actively control the game once it starts. Normally, one of the players is the team's leader. So, sports management isn't confused with leadership.

> Management and leadership are functions. Leadership generates new directions; management executes them.

Management organizes, coordinates and motivates skilled knowledge workers. Coaching, empowering and facilitating are management activities, not leadership. Routine work only needs to be monitored. But complex projects involving diverse stakeholders, such as putting the first man on the moon or making a complex movie, must be managed well. Such work is no routine factory operation.

Why is management despised?

Leadership is seen as uplifting, inspiring, nurturing, supporting, liberating, empowering and transformational. Management is viewed as controlling, mechanistic, bureaucratic, cold, transactional and punitive. Why?

This is partly Fredrick Taylor's fault for basing his model of management on the assembly-line with its robotic efficiency. Management suffered another setback when the West needed a scapegoat to take the blame for its lack of competitiveness in the face of the Japanese onslaught of the 1970s/80s. There was a great hue and cry from all quarters, including Jack Welch and Tom Peters, to replace managers with leaders. This was a gross error because it confused ends and means. The *end* of management is, like investment, to get the best return on all resources for a set goal. The *means* do not have to be controlling. Managers can be as empowering and inspiring as they need to be.

Abraham Zaleznik's trashing of management

We can thank the *Harvard Business Review* for keeping Abraham Zalesnik's vitriolic denunciation of management in front of us since its publication nearly 30 years ago (His 1977 article, *Managers and Leaders: Are they different?*).[1] In his later book, *The Managerial Mystique*, Frederick Taylor is Zaleznik's whipping boy: "what Taylor proposed through his system of management lies at the core of how modern managers are supposed to think and act. The principle is rationality. The aim is efficiency."[2] Zaleznik sees managers and leaders as having different personalities. Without questioning Taylor, Zaleznik sees managers as cold efficiency machines who "adopt impersonal, if not passive, attitudes towards goals."[3] Further "Managers see themselves as conservators and regulators of an existing order of affairs.[4]"

Zaleznik claims that "managers" tactics appear flexible: on the one hand they negotiate and bargain; on the other, they use rewards, punishments, and other forms of coercion."[5] Further "... one often hears subordinates characterize managers as inscrutable, detached and manipulative."[6] He doesn't tell us where he "often hears" these comments. Perhaps he spent a lot of time wandering around 1970s auto assembly plants where he would surely have run into the ghost of Frederick Taylor!

Zaleznik recognizes that managers talk to people, but they "maintain a low level of emotional involvement in those relationships."[7] They also "lack empathy".[8] Further, they "operate within a narrow range of emotions. This emotional blandness when combined with the preoccupation on process, leads to the impression that managers are inscrutable, detached and even manipulative."[9]

Zaleznik endorses Taylor's view of management without asking himself whether, as a function, it is committed to this damning portrayal. Starting with Taylor's worship of machine-like efficiency, Zaleznik has tarred all managers for all time with the same brush.

Writing at the height of the Japanese onslaught, Zaleznik's vitriol is understandable. But this whole nonsense is due to binary thinking. By focusing on persons in roles to define leadership we went down the dead end track of talking about initiating structure versus showing consideration and theory X (people need to be monitored) versus theory Y (people are responsible).

As already noted, leadership got the good guy role and management the bad guy part. But managers need to flip back and forth between both sides of the people versus task coin. Leadership has nothing to do with getting things done or maximizing performance so neither side of these pairings applies to leadership. Managers need to manage complex projects, not just monitor routine operations. Contrary to Zaleznik, they do not necessarily preserve the status quo either. They can be as change-friendly as leaders; they just don't *promote* change.

Warren Bennis's clever saying comes to mind: *Leaders do the right things. Managers do things right.*[10] The reality is that leaders do not DO anything. Like Martin Luther King, they champion new things. Managers need to do *both* the right things *and* things right.

Management as investment

In an excellent recent attempt to bring management back from the dead called *What Management Is*,[11] Joan Magretta equates management with organization "without organization of some sort, nothing would get done."[12] Hence, without management, we would achieve nothing. Magretta notes that Jack Welch "consciously rejected the word *manager*. It smacked of control and bureaucracy. Welch was on a crusade. His call for *leaders* struck a responsive chord."[12] Management has been in the rubbish dump ever since.

Magretta tells us that "Managers commit resources today, in the face of uncertainty to create the future. In other words, they must know how to invest..."[13]

Absolutely! Investment is a great way to view management. Successful investors shift their investments around to increase their return. Managers have personal resources: time, work experience, talent and energy to invest. They also invest organizational resources: people, a budget, material and various tools. The aim, end or function of management is to get the best return from all such resources relative to a particular goal.

> The means of making and getting best value from a manager's investments is profoundly different from what it was in Frederick Taylor's day.

Examples of management in action

Review the examples below and decide which ones are leadership and which management.

Leadership or management?	Mgt√	Lead√
1. Mary's team is demoralized because their performance targets have been increased and they feel they're unrealistic. Mary pulls them together to brainstorm how to develop smarter ways of working so their new targets become more achievable.		
2. Midway through the year, Mary's team are on target but stressed by the pace and workload. She delivers a stirring speech about how important their work is to the company vision, how well they're doing and what the future holds. They go back to work re-energized.		
3. Mary recognizes that a major product in her division is nearing the end of its life cycle but doesn't know what might replace it. She runs a brainstorming session with her team and they devise a new product. Mary then promotes it to her superiors.		
4. Being up to date technically and close to customers, Mary develops an idea for a new product on her own, sells it to her team, then to her superiors.		

Leadership or management?	Mgt√	Lead√
5. A customer suggests an idea for a new product which Mary then sells to her team and her superiors.		
6. Mary sees a way to reorganize her team to foster better cross-fertilization and convinces the team to adopt her idea.		
7. Mary finds one team member blocking communication and, failing to get him to change, removes him from the team.		
8. For 8 months Mary has an added role to manage a cross-functional team to launch a new product. Mary provides technical input but, as she has great communication and organizing skills, her main input is to keep everyone on the team working well until the new product is launched.		

My take on the Mary's actions

1. In the first example, Mary is in managerial mode because she's facilitating decision-making and creative thinking in others. Mary isn't championing any new directions. She acts as a coach or catalyst, asking questions to stimulate leadership in others.
2. Here again, Mary is engaged in managerial motivation to improve performance. Mary is managing, not advocating a new direction. She is just motivating her team to execute an existing direction with greater conviction and energy.
3. Mary is now operating as a manager in her team but showing leadership upward. With her team, although the focus is to generate new directions rather than to execute an existing one, Mary facilitates the discussion; she doesn't promote her own ideas. When she starts talking up the team's idea to her superiors, she

switches to upward leadership mode.
4. Here Mary shows thought leadership both down and up as she promotes her own idea in both directions.
5. The idea for a new product isn't Mary's but she shows leadership up and down by promoting it.
6. Mary shows leadership downward by selling a process change, rather than a change in products or services.
7. By firing a team member, Mary makes a management decision. No leadership is shown here.
8. Finally, Mary is again a manager with the cross-functional team. This example illustrates the point that managing a team isn't routine. It isn't monitoring a machine-like process that barely needs watching. Launching a new product is very complex, but the skills of organization and communication are managerial. Mary isn't showing leadership. Hence management defined as execution or implementation covers the most complex imaginable projects.

Did you identify number two as leadership, where Mary delivered a stirring speech to motivate her team? It's counterintuitive to classify cheerleading as management. This seems odd only because we're used to focusing on the whole *person* in charge of the group as the leader, not just the function. When we stick to the latter, then we must say that management is what is happening if the focus is execution, no matter how inspiring the manager is when influencing a team.

The function of management

Mary's actions show that leadership and management must be defined as functions, not as styles or types of persons.

Organizations have two very different tasks:

- To execute today's business in line with set goals.
- To create the future, to meet new demands.

Having two discrete tasks forces us to separate leadership and management just as we did with sales and marketing when business development became complex enough to demand distinct functions.

Traditionally, writers on leadership were fixated on the person at the head of a group, so they studied what notable leaders did. Their books are filled with the exploits of widely admired heroes. Studying examples of real leaders to determine the meaning of leadership suggests looking at personality differences. But suppose you were an alien from a distant planet sent here to learn what sort of thing is a Sales Director. Would you do research on a sample of Sales Directors? No, you would read up on organizational theory to find out what *function* Sales Directors perform and how their role differs from those of Human Resource, Marketing and Finance Directors. The only value in studying live Sales Directors would be to learn how effective ones differ from the less effective. Field research wouldn't tell you what it *means* to be a Sales Director in the first place. A Sales Director is simply someone who carries out the *function* of producing sales through managing the sales process and a sales team.

> *Management* serves the function of getting things done so as to get the best return on the investment of all resources.

What's new?

John Kotter[14] offered a functional distinction between leadership and management, but one stuck in the past. For Kotter: "... leadership and management differ in terms of their primary function. The first can produce useful change, the second can create orderly results which keeps something working efficiently."[15] But Kotter's account goes only half way, because he adds that leaders must be inspirational to fire up change while managers need only be machine-like controllers. Unfortunately, therefore, Kotter still clouds our efforts to differentiate leadership from management. He doesn't actually move much beyond Zaleznik's dismissal of managers.

This problem stems from studying people in charge. We wanted to learn how they could best motivate employees to perform. This led to the debate over whether it was better to initiate structure or show consideration for people, to be theory X or Y. The transformational-transactional option is just the same old question of whether to focus on the task or people. The reason Kotter's approach fails is that he doesn't fully break away from this old personality, style tradition. So, even though he states that leaders and managers serve different functions, he still believes leaders focus on people and are transformational while managers are taskmasters and transactional.

Worse, Kotter limits management to keeping routine operations ticking over, much like Frederick Taylor, rather than allowing them to get *everything* done no matter how complex the task. Managers, for Kotter, are controlling and uninspiring. Leaders both promote *and* manage change, he argues, by being transformational, inspiring and empowering. But, because he sees leaders as *implementing* change (not just championing it), he blurs the lines even further between leadership and management.

Surely, some aspects of managing change require good project management skills, not leadership. So the line between the two functions in Kotter's world is fuzzy. Kotter confuses ends and means by allowing only leaders to be transformational.

> A functional distinction between leadership and management leaves the *means* of moving people open simply because ends never imply any particular means.

This is important because Kotter is stuck with leadership-as-position. Leaders are people (not just functions) in positions of authority for Kotter, which is why he sees them as implementing, not just promoting, change. This rules out leading bottom-up or from the sidelines where the leader has no hand in execution. But bottom-up thought leadership is a vital source of competitive advantage that needs to be actively fostered. We must move beyond Kotter's confused distinction if we want a concept of leadership divorced from position, one that can be shown as readily bottom-up as top-down.

The Transformational Manager

Champions of transformational leadership theory, like Kotter, see both leaders and managers as striving to get the best out of people. This is because they have their eye on the person in charge, which leads us to look at that person's influencing style or personality to say how leadership and management differ. When you focus solely on function, it's clear that leaders and managers need to be transformational or inspirational, *only when followers show resistance*.

	1 Transformational leader	2 Simply point out new direction
Promote changes in direction		
Maintain productivity	3 Transformational manager	4 Monitor, communicate coordinate
	High resistance and task difficulty	Low resistance and task difficulty

In **Box 1**, leaders are striving to sell change. It helps to be transformational to meet strong resistance. They need to be highly convincing in their presentation of the rationale for change, hence inspiring, charismatic and visionary. This is the paradigm case of leadership for those who wrote about leadership starting in the 1980s when, following the traumas of the Japanese business invasion, major change was needed to save the day.

In **Box 2**, followers are opportunists, so ready to jump on the latest bandwagon that the leader merely has to point to an exciting new idea and stand aside. Recall Carlos with his spam blocking software whose followers needed no persuading to get on board with his idea. No transformational influencing skills were required in this instance. Here, leadership reduces to indicating a new direction that might yield a great leap in competitive advantage. This is like being a security guard in a burning building and saying "This way!" to the panicking occupants – they don't need much persuading to follow.

In **Box 3**, suppose a team is falling behind schedule on its targets as in our example where Mary needed to re-motivate her team. Here the manager recognizes that the work is hard, the task is complex and not very exciting. She also sees that her team isn't especially inspired. To motivate a higher level of performance, she makes her team see how special they'll be if they can beat the odds and make their deadline. The way the manager explains the importance of the work and how much she values their efforts is quite transformational or inspiring. Because no new direction is advocated, the manager isn't showing leadership. Still, she is such an inspiring motivator, that she is transformational. Very complex projects like putting a man on the moon for the first time are also in this box. It doesn't contain merely routine operational work.

In **Box 4**, the manager's team is already highly motivated and determined to reach its targets. Now, the manager doesn't need to be transformational because the team is already motivated enough. Perhaps they just enjoy a challenge or maybe they're in line for a bonus. In any case, the manager's task is just one of coordination to ensure that all team members pull in the same direction.

The moral of this story is that *employee resistance*, the *complexity of the task* and the *magnitude of change* determine whether managers and leaders need to be transformational. It isn't a matter of the leader having a transformational personality while the manager is a controlling drone. Both need to be transformational to overcome resistance, one to move people to change direction, and the other to get them there efficiently. This is the inescapable conclusion of defining leadership and management strictly in functional terms.

What managers do

For industries that compete primarily through cost, service and quality rather than innovation, it's all about execution. The banking industry is typical, as Sandy Weill, former CEO of Citigroup, explains "In our business, no one has unique products. We're very focused on the bottom line and how efficient we can be in delivering our product."[16] Efficient delivery is the essence of management, but that doesn't mean being cold, controlling and mechanistic. Industries that need a constant stream of new products, on top of efficient execution, need both leadership and management to succeed. The leadership may or may not come mainly from the top.

Airlines are in the same boat. They innovate around the edges but compete primarily through good service and value for money. Herb Kelleher is famous for creating a culture at Southwest Airlines where "people can really enjoy what they're doing."[17] Championing a *new* culture is a leadership act but sustaining it is just good management.

Managers have highly skilled, self-managing human resources to invest. Engaging employees in thinking about *what* needs to be done, as well as *how* to do it, is a facilitative activity. The best way to engage employees' brains is to ask them open questions:

- What goals should we aim for?
- How can you best add value to these aims?
- What options do you see to meet our targets?
- What are the pros and cons of your options?
- What new opportunities can you see on the horizon?
- What threats can you envisage?
- What new ideas have you got from anyone lately?
- What support from me would be most helpful?
- Who else do you think should be involved?
- How does this impact other parts of the business?

Managers act as catalysts by asking good questions. They aim to generate better decisions but also to foster greater ownership in their teams. Stimulating questions also develop employees. The key point is that acting as a coach or catalyst isn't showing leadership.

Good to Great – "level 5 leaders" as managers

A brilliant testimony to management's resurgence is the work of Jim Collins as reported in *Good to Great*.[18] While Collins doesn't differentiate leadership from management, his "level 5 leaders" can be seen as managers. The chief executives Collins cites appear to follow the 80-20 rule – spending the bulk of their time managing (facilitating) and much less leading as I characterize it – personally advocating their own ideas.

Consistent with their modesty, feeling that they did not have the answers, the *Good to Great* Chief executives got their stars together and asked challenging questions to draw new strategies out of them. They didn't promote their own visions. Their approach was facilitative to get the best thinking out of their teams. Because they didn't promote their own strategies they didn't show leadership. "Level 5" leadership is just a perverse shifting of the goal posts, redefining leadership to save the conventional image of the person in charge as the leader when it becomes clear that he or she no longer actually provides direction.

Conclusion

Management means getting things done efficiently through people. Management and leadership are both functions but only management is a role. Leadership is a bit like creativity in not being something you can assign or direct people to do. You can hold people accountable for managing work, but not for being creative. You can only foster and support creativity. The same is true of leadership. Like creativity, it is a function, but not a role or position and it can only be fostered. The phrase "senior leadership team" is a misnomer. The correct label is senior management or executive team. You can't appoint anyone to a leadership position because there are none. "Leadership position" is as much an oxymoron as "military intelligence".

Managers, unlike leaders, have responsibilities because of the authority they have over people and other resources. Getting the best out of these resources calls for organizational and motivational skills but especially for the open questioning used by the catalyst and coach as outlined above. Most importantly, managers can be inspiring in their motivational style. They can also be empowering and caring. They're not restricted to mechanical control and transactional rewards to motivate people.

The aim of this chapter has been to bring management back from the dead, to make it a constructive function. Organizations like those studied by Jim Collins in *Good to Great* can be very successful with excellent management. It's time to recognize managers as the heroes they are. It isn't only leadership that is heroic. Now that I have reframed management, I turn in the next chapter to fleshing out my view of leadership.

Tom Bower's questions and my replies

Tom Bower asked me

"Are you saying that leaders don't take charge?"

"I'm saying that *people* take charge wearing two hats. First they promote something new, showing leadership. Wearing a managerial hat, they stay involved to make sure their idea is acted on."

"I can see how you're making management a more positive force, but why should this matter to me in my business?"

"Because you value your time. To get the best return from all your efforts, you need to know when leadership is required and when management is called for. If you delude yourself into thinking that you're always showing leadership just by motivating people to perform well, your business might be losing out on the real leadership it needs to stay ahead of your competitors. Also, if you monopolize leadership, you own too much while everyone else depends on you. As a result, they make too little effort to champion better ways of doing things."

"What does it matter as long as things get done properly?"

"Because beating the competition today requires more than just getting things done well. You need to be constantly reinventing yourself. To engage people fully in this much harder task, you need to share the leadership stage with them. If you own the whole territory of figuring out how to improve your business, you can't hope to be as successful as you want. The world is too complex and fast changing for you to do all the new thinking. It's like differentiating between sales and marketing. We didn't need this level of specialization when business was simple. Separating sales and marketing was driven by complexity. Today, all organizations have two very different tasks: to deliver today's results as well as possible and to create the future. This calls for two separate functions."

"So what's new? Haven't we always had a good enough distinction between leadership and management?"

"Absolutely not! It's been totally confused, clouded by too many myths about the real nature of leadership. I explain more of this in the next chapter."

CHAPTER 3

The Sharp Edge of Leadership

WHAT DOES IT TAKE to *become* a leader? What about *being* a leader? Or *showing* leadership?
I asked these questions of John Wells. He explained

"I find it odd to talk of either *becoming* or *being* a leader. For me, it's like being *in* the lead in a football league or half way through a golf tournament. It's something you do or achieve temporarily, not something you are, either because of the sort of person you are or the role you occupy."

I replied "We do talk of a golfer being in the lead, John, but what has that got to do with leading a team?"

"If you were a reporter asking Tiger Woods, leading midway through a tournament, how he became such a great leader, don't you think you would draw a blank?"

"I see what you mean. A good golfer has superior golf skills, not leadership skills. It's only through golf skills that someone becomes, however briefly, in the lead."

"Yes, that's it. We *show* leadership through other skills. When I ranted and raved about our obsolete products and pushed new ideas, I knew what I was talking about and I spoke with conviction. We can call that showing leadership as a short-hand, but that doesn't make me a leader in any ongoing sense, not as I see it anyway."

John is saying is that displaying leadership is an act, a selling of ideas not a role. And because no one has a monopoly on good ideas, showing leadership is very temporary, fleeting, ephemeral, unlike holding onto the top slot in a hierarchy, which is intended to be a stable state.

But there must be something about some people that disposes them to show leadership which other people lack. What is that something?

First of all, it isn't as much of an inherent personal trait as you might think. Recall my example of Jim brainstorming in his auto assembly team. Jim did not *bring* leadership to the table. He was stimulated by brainstorming in two ways:

- He got an idea he might never have had otherwise.
- Because someone initially laughed at his idea, he got angry and expressed himself much more forcefully than he ever did at work before or since.

Jim's display of leadership was totally contextual, a one-off. After the meeting, he went back to being a quiet, efficient but unemotional worker with little to say about how the work should be done.

Let's look at what Jim *did* in the meeting then if we can't learn much from examining his personality traits. What are the two things he did that made a difference?

- He discovered something worth saying.
- He had the courage to promote his idea with conviction.

This sounds just like what John Wells did. He had something to say and he was provoked to say it with blazing, white hot passion.

Having something to say requires a unique perspective on a specific subject, even if you gain it spontaneously in the heat of debate with colleagues or customers. The second quality, having the courage of your convictions, could also arise unexpectedly, say if you're provoked to express yourself more passionately than usual. Moreover, leadership isn't all-or-nothing. It can range, as we have seen, from advocating small changes in operating procedures to radically new business concepts.

We need to look at these two key factors in a bit more detail. First, having something worthwhile to say and, then, having the courage to say it.

Substance or form – something worth saying

Conventional leadership revolves around powerful influencing skills Aspiring chief executives must be very persuasive to rise to the top. More primitively, all animals form hierarchies. What counts in the animal kingdom is physical strength, a more basic form of power than the force of personality, but the aim is the same: to attain dominance through powerful influencing ability.

It almost doesn't matter *what* such leaders have to say or where they want to take us. We follow them if they have enough power, presence or charisma to seduce us. This is why we expect all manner of wisdom from movie stars and pop music heroes when they're interviewed by the media. We think that anyone with such power must have some striking insight into the way the world works.

This phenomenon is the triumph of form over substance. But we're now in the midst of an epoch-making transition to a knowledge based existence. It isn't the *possession* or use of knowledge that counts. It's the ability to generate new practical knowledge, applications that have value in the eyes of consumers. This is why we now need a concept of leadership that is knowledge based. So, we're moving from the power of brute strength and the force of personality to the power of new ideas as the basis for leadership. The conventional leader aims to dominate us. The thought leader can't achieve this aim because the power to generate new knowledge can't be monopolized and such people are not often interested in power anyway.

> Thought leadership: the triumph of substance over form.

Substance equals new ideas. *Form* is the way people express their views about what directions we should pursue. We're in an era where substance counts – as in evidence-based decision making in the health care sector and other scientific or high-tech markets where innovation is the paramount source of competitive advantage. Form isn't irrelevant but it's no longer central, no longer the essence of leadership. This is because some good ideas can be sold by example, even though many will clearly have to be promoted actively. Form is now only the means of expressing leadership.

In the words of Gary Hamel: "Inventing new *whats* – that's the key to thriving in the age of revolution."[1]

We describe our age as one of complexity, rapid change and hyper-competition. But the motor is rapid innovation, better ideas. Innovation generates complexity directly in terms of a bewildering array of choices but also through multiple ways in which organizations can collaborate to create and deliver new services or products. This isn't to say that ideas alone are sufficient to lead people. They can be, in some circumstances, but generally they require explicit influencing effort (form), which can range from hard evidence bluntly delivered to a visionary, emotionally arousing speech.

Complexity and rapid change render direction from remote generals impossible. Hence why we have guerrilla warfare. New ideas emerge, not from an ivory tower, but in the midst of interactions among front-line employees and customers or users. To the extent that leadership provides direction and it emerges from the front-lines instead of from the top, then leadership is bottom-up. Influencing style (form) can vary too widely to be part of the meaning of leadership. Because thought leadership aims only to change how we think, not to dominate the group, and because better ideas are often evidence-based, the definitional link between influencing style and leadership is broken.

It isn't that influencing skills are unimportant. It's just that they become the *means*, the tools or the vehicle of leadership, no longer its essence. Influencing skills were only the core of leadership when it was defined as having what it takes to get to the top of a hierarchy or to inspire major change. We might still want generals to inspire major campaigns but today this image misses the real nature of the everyday leadership that occurs on all fronts, all the time, all around us.

The courage to speak – Are leaders born?

Courage is an inherent trait, like being strong or tall, but it's also a type of motivation. People who show courage must *want* to take the risks associated with dangerous actions.

Often younger people are the most courageous, just as they're more creative and rebellious. Courage in a young person is partly due to having less to lose than mature people who often have more invested in their careers. But the young are also more driven to make their mark, to differentiate themselves, to challenge authority, and find a better way. We fall along a continuum from being very rebellious at one end of the scale to wanting to be accepted by a group, to belong, at the other end of the spectrum. It's hard to argue that some people are more naturally willing to stick their necks out, to take higher risks, to be readier to risk group rejection than others. It's also evident that such courage develops naturally, like youthful rebelliousness; hence it isn't a learned skill set.

The *content* that forms the substance of a thought leadership attempt is, of course, learned. So are influencing skills. While emotional intelligence isn't essential to show leadership, having it can better enable thought leaders to brainstorm successfully with colleagues and influence upward more persuasively if they have bosses who see themselves as the fount of wisdom. Youthful rebelliousness is the *potential* to lead, just as having a talent for music or art is a potential that may or may not be realized. It's this potential to lead that people are born with, but this doesn't mean that there are born leaders.

People who seem to be born orators are easily classed as born leaders, but in a knowledge-driven age, there is no advantage in being able to speak compellingly if you have nothing worth saying. This is like taking viagra without a partner. The key to leadership in today's high-tech world is a combination of content and the courage to promote it. Being a great orator is a nice add-on rather than an essential element. This means that the basis of leadership is as biological as ever but we need to switch the emphasis from the urge to dominate a hierarchy to the drive to differentiate oneself – the desire shared by artists, scientists and other achievers. The difference between being a competent professional and being a leader in your field is based on an unlearned motivation to differentiate yourself, to say something new and distinctive that leaves a lasting mark on your peers and perhaps the world at large.

Benefits of leadership recast as unlearnable

It isn't politically correct to claim that leadership can't be learned. Worse, it sounds disempowering because it seems to imply that only the privileged few can show leadership. But you only get this impression if your models of leadership are larger-than-life characters like Abraham Lincoln, Napoleon or Churchill. The truth is that everyone already shows leadership every time he or she suggests doing something different. Leaders are pioneers: they go somewhere new. Being the first to explore the Amazon jungle makes the headlines but everyone does something new every day.

Conventional leadership theory is wrong and damaging on three counts. First it holds up impossible acts to follow as the paradigm cases of leadership, then it defines leadership in terms of powerful, inspiring influencing skills and, finally, it says anyone can learn to be like that. Even if we agree with this definition, it's by no means clear that quiet, shy introverts can transform themselves into a Churchill or a Jack Welch. So, the claim that leadership so defined can be learned is a lie, one that everyone sees through. This self-deception makes leadership an even more remote possibility for many.

Redefining leadership as promoting anything new, regardless of how small, is liberating because it's done by everyone every day. Leadership admits of degrees just as does being a pioneer. The fact that we most admire pioneering or leadership acts at the heroic end of the scale should not rule out smaller scale, everyday acts of leadership by definition.

> Ironically, saying leadership can't be learned is *more* liberating than saying it can be if we define it as something everyone can do now instead of as having the power to ascend a hierarchy.

This isn't to say that everyone can show leadership. Those who are especially risk-averse or threat-sensitive might strenuously avoid sticking their necks out, but many more people can show leadership than can rise to significant positions of authority in a group.

The question of what can be developed and how leadership can be fostered is discussed in greater depth in Chapter Six.

What leaders do

When you show leadership, do you set direction for your team? Do you move them along the path to a destination?

If you answer "yes" to the second question, you're wearing a managerial hat. But what about the first question? The difficult word here is "set". Does it mean that you *decide* direction or *promote* it?

In simpler times when we said that leaders set direction, we meant that they *decided* it. But making decisions is an exercise of authority and only people in formal roles have this power. If showing leadership doesn't mean occupying a role, then setting direction must mean selling, not deciding, it. In fact, from this point of view, all executive *decisions* are managerial. Leadership is strictly about the *promotion* of new directions.

Thanks to complexity, we must be open to new directions from wherever they arrive. So, leadership is *proposing* directions rather than deciding them. Only those with the power to decide can do so, but they might be led to their decisions by people without that power, knowledge workers who can only make proposals.

This places executives in the role of a customer or venture capitalist, someone who chooses between alternative proposals, but this is a *response* to leadership, hence followership. Being thus on the receiving end of leadership, and having the power to decide, requires sound management judgement rather than leadership. While this might seem upside down, it makes sense of thought leadership but also links up nicely with the leadership of Martin Luther King who could only make proposals, not decide direction, for his target group, the U.S. government.

These ideas fly in the face of our mainstream conception of leadership. In his popular textbook, *Leadership in Organizations*, Gary Yukl tells us that "The most commonly used measure of leader effectiveness is the extent to which the leader's organizational unit performs its task successfully and attains its goals."[2] This popular model of leadership views the output of leadership as task accomplishment. It's precisely this idea that we need to question. No doubt people in charge get groups to achieve goals, but they can wear two hats enroute.

Consider an example where a team meets informally to solve a problem. They have two decisions to make: What is the best solution and how should they implement it? There's no formal leader in the meeting, but George is more confident, talkative, decisive and experienced than the others. He's also more organized, hence better able to set out a viable implementation plan. Although most team members throw in a few ideas on both questions – what to do and how to do it, they eventually defer to George. He doesn't insist on his way but he's so forceful and confident that the others just see him as the natural leader and, sooner or later, defer to his preferences.

One of the team members, Sarah, is brighter than George and she regularly reads up on new practices in their field. In some of their meetings, George and the rest of the team follow the lead of Sarah because she presents compelling evidence that her solution will be more workable than George's. Sarah isn't very talkative, assertive, decisive or confident, but she can articulate a case for her ideas very clearly. But, even on these occasions, George usually sets out the implementation plan. After the meeting, George is most active in directing implementation.

Who is showing leadership in this team and how?

George's contribution is a mix of three elements:

- Some good ideas on what to do, genuine leadership.
- Managerial – organizational ideas for implementation.
- Traditional leadership – old fashioned dominance based on the force of his personality.

When the team is influenced by Sarah, it's because she shows genuine leadership but none of the traditional dominance traits. And because she's not organized, she doesn't say much on how to implement the chosen solution.

The question now is: Why are we so strongly inclined to regard George as the team's primary informal leader?

I think it's partly because we're programmed to defer to dominant personalities, which is why we robotically form ourselves into hierarchies just like so many other higher animals. Also, we're impressed by people who know how to implement a solution in an organized manner. But suppose we strip away the organizational skills and dominance. What's left? Only thought leadership and management. Even then we might still see George as the informal leader because he takes charge of implementation and comes up with his share of thought leadership. No doubt George does show some genuine leadership, but in simple situations like this, we fail to differentiate it from positional leadership, just as we don't bother to separate sales from marketing in small businesses.

In a knowledge-driven age, more leadership is like Sarah's and we can no longer let ourselves be swayed solely by the power of personality (pure form) to move us. Substance is now more important. Further, because complexity generates greater specialization, we need to make the effort to separate management from the genuine leadership that Sarah shows and George too occasionally.

The upshot here is that getting tasks done is at least 80 percent management and 20 percent leadership. When it's unclear what to do, there's room for *content* leadership. When the objective or task is clear and it remains only to decide how to organize implementation; some *process* leadership helps, but the bulk of the driving force behind getting things done is good management.

Leadership shown by executives

So far I've banged the drum about how non-managers can show leadership, but what about executives? Which of the following examples would you count as leadership? Which ones would you view as management?

1. Jim heads up a major bank and is known for his efforts to change the culture of the organization to make it a best place to work.
2. Lynn runs a charity and has a reputation for devising new avenues for raising money. She tests out ideas in one area before promoting them across the organization. Lynn isn't very good at managing people as she is so often out of the office.
3. As Chief executive, David's business is tops in profitability. He has a knack for motivating everyone to

pay close attention to costs and customers.
4. When Anne was brought into run a consulting firm, she made it her top priority to promote high ethical standards for dealing with customers, employees and financial information.
5. Phil has always been an excellent troubleshooter and he still puts this skill to good use now that he is Chief executive. Phil is very creative in devising unique solutions to complex problems and in selling his solutions to the organization.
6. Tom is a Sales Director, one of the most charismatic in his industry. He excels in motivating his sales force to exceed targets. Because he spends a lot of time with customers, Tom often picks up ideas for new products which he then champions to the Board.

Are all of these executives leaders? Assume they're all successful and widely admired.

1. Jim's efforts to promote a new culture count as *process* leadership. He isn't advocating new products or services, but he is pushing to change how things are done. Jim isn't personally innovative and his ideas have long been in use elsewhere, but he does show leadership to his organization because he champions ideas that were not in place before he started promoting them.
2. Lynn also shows leadership. She is personally creative and enjoys coming up with new ways to improve results. She doesn't impose her ideas on the organization but she's so persuasive that she doesn't need to make unilateral decisions. Her deputy looks after the people and internal processes. Because Lynn devises new services, not just new ways of delivering existing ones, she shows *content* leadership.
3. David displays excellent management skills, not leadership. He excels at getting the best out of people. Because the organization is working well, there's no need to champion major change. David is ideal for the

job because he's in a people business and the requirement is for someone skilled at coaching and empowering people. His contribution is managerial because his focus is on excellent execution, making the best use of all resources he has to invest.
4. Anne is showing a different form of process leadership by promoting new values and ethical standards. Anne is a skilled promoter but also an empowering manager. She needs to be because she doesn't personally enjoy the detail of implementation. Her leadership revolves around vision and inspiration.
5. Phil doesn't promote new directions, neither new processes nor new products. But he shows leadership by championing creative solutions to problems. Notice that this isn't the same as if he simply solved problems and implemented them himself. Again, he doesn't care to implement his ideas. He's a troubleshooter who, once he sees a solution to a problem, launches a roadshow to sell it to others.
6. Tom, the Sales Director, doesn't show leadership when motivating his team to sell. Despite his obvious charisma, his focus is on performance, executing existing targets, not on promoting new directions. Still, he does shift into leadership mode when he spots a new product idea. On these occasions, his leadership is initially lateral and upward to get his senior colleagues on board. This example is counterintuitive but it's essential to see that influencing style isn't a marker of leadership. Leaders and managers can be either charismatic or quiet. They're differentiated only on the basis of their function, purpose or aim.

The bottom line for leadership reborn

- Leadership is no longer bloated and diffuse, covering everything under the sun relating to getting things done through people.

- It's now focused on promoting new directions and nothing else.
- Leadership is more sharply differentiated from management as a function with no reference to style of moving people.
- Management is reinstated as a vital and positive force for enabling employees to achieve their potential.
- The main requirements to show leadership are having something worthwhile to say and the courage to say it.
- Polished influencing skills are nice to have and will help you win some people over, but the most critical factor is the strength of your conviction. It's vital to use whatever influencing method works with your target audience. Some will fall for an emotional appeal. Others will want the facts, hard evidence.
- Leadership is like guerrilla warfare, free-floating initiatives that anyone can launch from anywhere, the front-lines of organizations, the top or the sidelines. It isn't a fixed role.
- What used to be called "informal leadership" is really informal management because it refers to non-managers taking charge and organizing implementation. All leadership is informal in the sense that all influence not based on formal authority is informal.
- Emotional intelligence, integrity and character are vital for people in responsible positions. But leadership isn't a position, so having such traits falls under the heading of influencing style (for leaders) which, of course, is situational – sometimes they're needed, sometimes not. Such qualities are not definitional for leadership.
- Leadership has nothing to do with making decisions with or for a group. Only managers make decisions. This means that there is no such thing as either participative or autocratic leadership. These adjectives apply only to management. When a decision is made on a fully participative basis with no one taking a stand on anything, then no leadership has occurred.

Benefits of leadership reborn

- Executives can be more strategic in deploying their resources, knowing when they're leading and when they're managing.
- All employees not in managerial positions can show leadership upward and sideways without waiting to be promoted. Their level of empowerment and engagement goes up several notches.
- Organizations that see the link between engagement and retention will steal a march in the talent wars.
- Businesses that depend on innovation can encourage all employees to come forward without fear if they have new ideas to promote.
- Senior executives can be effective by being good managers even if they find it difficult to show leadership. Their organizations might not need new products, services or processes. Or they might be better at getting things done than driving the new.

Tom Bower's questions and my replies

Tom wondered

"What's the meaning of leadership style in your view?"

"What used to be meant by leadership style, how the person in charge makes decisions, participatively or unilaterally, or how delegation is handled, is really management style. There's no such thing as leadership style. There's influencing style but this is quite different from what we used to mean by leadership style."

"If you mean that I can't be seen as an autocratic leader anymore, I'm pleased to hear that!"

"If you make decisions autocratically, you can still be an autocratic manager. Leadership has nothing to do with making decisions."

"OK. What about the leadership principle of taking people with you during major change? Is this leadership or management?"

"It's a bit of both. Wearing a leadership hat, you promote a new direction or vision and maybe resell it a few times enroute. But management is at least as important. It's everything facilitative you do to involve people in planning and implementing the change. Asking questions to learn people's concerns and get their suggestions is a way of managing, not leading. What you're doing is managing a group process of generating a joint decision on how to proceed with your vision. Management also covers any anxiety-reducing things you say and do."

"But if I'm asking people questions, am I not leading a discussion?"

"Yes, but here 'leading' is used in a sloppy way, because it's confused with facilitating or chairing a meeting. We also refer to tour guides as 'leading the way' but this is like a trainer showing people how to do things. This is not really leadership as we need to think about it in a competitive business world or even in the public sector where there's constant pressure to offer new services or improve the delivery of existing ones. It's precisely because 'leadership' is used in so many loose ways that we should make an extra effort to be precise."

"That reminds me. Is all leadership thought leadership? Or are these different animals in your world?"

"Good question. Promoting a change in values doesn't amount to advocating new ideas. Also, when military commanders lead a charge against the enemy, they literally go first, so this is also not thought leadership. But all types of leadership involve promoting a new direction, even if only by example. No leadership involves managing implementation. My focus here is on organizations that need constant innovation and process improvement to stay relevant to their customers. In a war of ideas, the most urgently needed leadership is thought leadership."

"A lot of people these days are saying that all employees can show leadership. What's so different about your notion of thought leadership?"

"So-called *dispersed* leadership is just informal leadership repackaged for a new generation. It's still a jumble of management and leadership elements because informal leaders take charge to get things done. Leadership, as I define it, is totally purged of all managerial elements."

Still not convinced, Tom said "I'm confused. Winston Churchill is the leader I most admire but his leadership was not about questioning authority. Also, he made a lot of good decisions and kept British morale up during the war. Are you saying he was just a manager?"

"No. He showed leadership when he argued for action to stop Hitler, when he promoted new ways of waging war, and when he pushed to get the Americans involved. He also got involved in running the war effort on a day to day basis. Here he was wearing a managerial hat."

"Okay, but what about the way he kept everyone's spirits up during the bombing of London?"

"I'm glad you asked that because the whole business of soothing the anxieties of people is certainly a core element of our traditional image of the leader. In the chapter after next I argue that this paternal image of leadership is counterproductive and obsolete. People do like to look up to someone and have their anxieties appeased, but this can be seen as a managerial function."

Where next?

The next step is to address the question of how senior executives add value when they aren't leading. If we can't call them leaders just because they're effective, what exactly is their contribution?

Like Tom Bower, you might feel a nagging suspicion that something critical is left out of my account. This is our natural disposition to want one person at the head of affairs, someone to look up to who can help us cope with confusion and anxiety. Isn't this what we really mean by leadership?

When political leaders visit a disaster zone and call for calm, when they show themselves to be concerned and do something to resolve the crisis, or at least show they care, we feel gratified. This is an ancient way of looking at leadership, but it's riddled with paternalism. What place does such an image of leadership have in a knowledge-driven age? This is the subject of the chapter after next.

CHAPTER 4

What Executives Do If Not Lead

MANAGERS CAN NOW be seen in a brighter light because they:

- Do more than just keep operations ticking over.
- Do not just preserve the status quo.
- Can be receptive to change. They just don't promote it.
- Switch to wearing a leadership hat when they do promote change.
- Can be inspiring, empowering, and nurturing.
- Assume heroic levels of responsibility.
- Display integrity and emotional intelligence.
- Execute complex tasks efficiently.

The claim that executives are not automatically leaders just because they're effective is a threat to their identity and status. So, it's a good idea to look closely at what an executive can usefully get up to when not leading. As an executive, you want to invest your scarce personal resources in a way that gives you and your employer the best possible return, another reason to look carefully at what executives do when not showing leadership.

What executive activities give you the most satisfaction?

- Making strategic decisions
- Seeing others perform to their full potential
- Achieving targets

- Negotiating deals
- Being a role model
- Organizing and coordinating people
- Building organizational capability
- Coming up with new products
- Drawing good ideas out of others

I asked John Wells this question. He said,

> "I really like *doing* stuff, especially coming up with new product ideas and dealing with tough customer problems. I guess I'm a doer at heart."

"Nothing wrong with that, John," I replied, "but what do you do to get the best out of your team?"

> "That's a problem for me. As a role model, my message isn't very managerial. I'm conveying the impression that people at my level immerse themselves in the interesting stuff, just delegating menial tasks to underlings. I know it's not a positive image, but I'm working to change it."

"What are you trying to do differently, John?"

> "The key thing I'm doing now is spending more time with my people asking stimulating questions to draw ideas out of them. This way, I engage them instead of making all the interesting decisions myself."

John is aware that he isn't a natural manager, that he prefers to lead. But he's taking on board his responsibility to develop his team and get the best return he can from them. This is forcing him to think about other roles he can play to be a more rounded manager. His efforts to ask stimulating questions make him a coach or catalyst, a good way of managing, one that has nothing to do with leadership.

What executives do

Nine executive functions can be grouped under three headings: managing, doing and leading.

1. MANAGING

Investor – allocate and monitor resources for best return, drive execution, motivate performance.

Catalyst – facilitate decision making, be a broker, bring the right people together, resolve conflict, foster cross-functional working.

Coach – develop staff, promote learning, be a mentor, ask engaging questions to enhance confidence in others.

Steward – maintain a consistent culture and values, be a figurehead, manage anxiety, foster a best place to work

Architect – build or shape organizational capability, initiate judicious partnerships or acquisitions.

2. DOING

Promoter – represent and sell the organization to external stakeholders, negotiate important deals.

Expert – act as expert in a core competence, be an internal consultant, apply technical expertise.

3. LEADING

Content leader – champion new products, services, strategies, markets, new WHATS.

Process leader – champion new processes, cultures, ways of working, improve HOWS.

Strategic self-management and MANAGING

The first question is how to decide where to invest the bulk of your time to add most value. To manage yourself strategically means setting aside time regularly to review your priorities to see how best to deploy your personal resources. Investing your time wisely takes the same discipline you would use to monitor and shift your financial investments around.

1. MANAGING

Here you want the best return on all organizational resources: money, material and people. The Investor puts everything in its proper place and makes sure it works as it should. The Catalyst coordinates collaborative efforts across the group while the Coach develops individuals and teams to maximize their potential. The Steward provides the emotional glue that sustains a productive culture.

The Investor

When you operate as an Investor, you do the same thing with the organization's resources that you do when you manage yourself strategically: deploy people, material, time, talent, finance and energy and any other organizational resources at your disposal.

To invest wisely, you need to be sufficiently disciplined to set aside time to review your investments regularly. It also requires using the best means available to monitor your investments and measure their return. Prompt and accurate feedback is essential for making appropriate adjustments in how resources are deployed. This entails using a sophisticated system for obtaining information.

To get the best return out of human resources calls for more than slotting the right people in the right places and giving them the proper tools. You need to motivate them as well. This is nothing new. The important point is to see that this isn't leadership.

The Catalyst

The Catalyst, like the Investor, wants the best return out of all resources. As a Catalyst, you bring the right people together, like a broker or go-between. You decide what people to involve and what questions to ask to stimulate cross-functional sharing and synergy.

Catalysts help teams and organizations address what Ronald Heifetz[1] calls adaptive challenges. An adaptive challenge is an obstacle for which people are completely unprepared. To the extent that managers facilitate group brainstorming to devise solutions to such challenges, they're acting as Catalysts, not leaders. They lead only if they propose solutions themselves to tackle adaptive challenges.

Effective Catalysts do more than ask open, stimulating questions and draw people together. They're also supportive, never shooting down people or ridiculing ideas that, on the surface, seem a bit odd. Being supportive includes pointing to aspects of someone's proposal that you like before asking further, non-judgemental questions about aspects that you're not so sure are well-founded. Because Catalysts don't provide direction, they don't lead. Because they stimulate leadership in others, they strive to generate the best possible return on the organization's investment in people. This is a managerial mandate.

The goal of the Catalyst is to foster better decisions, including better operational performance and innovation. To facilitate the former, the Catalyst asks questions designed to stimulate problem-solving around a particular operational problem. To foster innovation, the emphasis is on stimulating creative thinking. You could call the provision of training and money for product development facilitation. But here we overlap with the Investor function.

The Coach

Coach and Catalyst skills are similar. Both ask questions to stimulate thinking in others. But the latter works on the organization, on group dynamics. As a Catalyst focusing on individuals, you're interested in fostering better decisions. The Coach, by contrast, *develops* people, both individuals and teams. At times, you wear both hats simultaneously, such as when you ask questions to develop employees *and* foster better decisions. In meetings where the team is fully developed, your questions serve only the Catalyst's aim, not to develop the team further.

The Catalyst has a broader focus than the Coach because of the goal of improving coordination. The Coach is strictly a developer of people – individuals and teams.

The Steward

The Steward manages the emotional climate of the group. This includes upholding the organization's core values, being positive in the face of uncertainty and supporting policies relating to employee wellbeing and job satisfaction. The Steward sustains the culture. Promoting *improvements* in a culture is *process leadership*. The Steward is a figurehead, someone to look up to for guidance in the midst of uncertainty, someone who offers emotional support. The Steward fosters harmony, not to stifle conflict, but just to maintain a productive level of cohesion. The Steward sounds like a conventional leader, but leadership, as defined here, is only the promotion of change.

2. DOING

Many executives enjoy *doing* things, working IN the business more than ON the business. They like using their knowledge, experience and analytical ability to make decisions such as to acquire companies, negotiate deals with customers or use their functional expertise to solve problems. Many executives actually don't enjoy working through others except in the sense of using the specialist expertise of others to help them make decisions themselves.

The Architect

The Architect has two aims – to make strategic decisions and to build organizations in line with evolving strategies. Making strategic decisions is different from influencing others to adopt them. The latter counts as leadership, but the making of such decisions isn't. Offering a vision could be either a management decision or a leadership proposal depending on whether it's made or sold to stakeholders.

The second aim is to shape organizational capability by re-structuring, adding divisions, expanding geographically or acquiring other companies. The reason this activity is Doing rather than Leading is that the executive decides unilaterally to carry out changes. If an executive *sells* the need for them instead, then this is leadership. But, in many cases, Chief executives only lead their immediate senior team. They then decide and thereby show no leadership to the rest of the organization.

The Promoter

Promoting the organization to external stakeholders is a Doing function and only incidentally a display of leadership. Wherever such activity is business as usual, no leadership is shown. Only where it's a novel action can it be called leadership – by example. But promoting the organization to stock brokers, shareholders or customers on an ongoing basis is a Doing activity. Promoters enjoy making deals with major customers, strategic partners, suppliers and other external stakeholders. They like to speak at conferences, address the media and generally be the public face of their organizations.

The Expert

Like the Promoter, Experts would rather use their expertise to make decisions than facilitate the thinking of others. Bill Gates is a little like this. When he decided to focus more on technology, he gave the Chief executive role to Martin Ballmer. Doers need to have sufficient emotional intelligence to recognize that someone else must tend to the other executive functions. When Experts solve a problem and unilaterally decide on a solution, they're in Doing mode. They show leadership only if they strive to sell their solutions to stakeholders.

3. LEADING

There are two leadership domains: content and process, the former to promote new products, services or markets and the latter to champion better processes, new ways of delivering existing products or services.

Content and Process leadership

Consider the following circles:

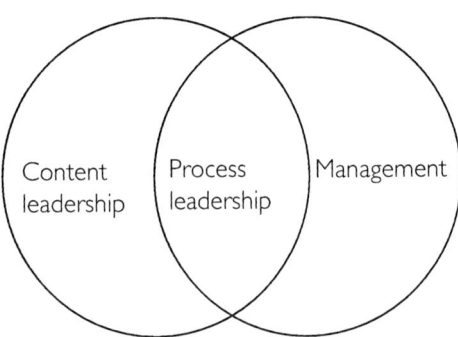

Process leadership is in the middle because of its dual emphasis on the leader's agenda to promote the new and the manager's aim to get things done efficiently.

Content leaders who are senior executives spend most of their time thinking about strategy, new products and new markets. How the organization operates isn't the main interest for those whose major strength is content leadership. Executives who are good at management are implementers. They excel in getting things done. They coordinate and communicate to resolve conflict and to get everyone pulling in the same direction. Process leaders have a foot in both camps. On the managerial side, they maintain efficiency, but as process leaders, they look for ways to improve that efficiency.

The merit of this distinction is to make it absolutely clear what counts as content leadership. One of the biggest problems with conventional leadership is that a leader is portrayed as doing anything and everything that makes an organization successful. Too many things count as leadership, leaving executives with no clear focus on where to place their emphasis. This isn't being strategic.

Jack Welch – leader or manager?

Jack Welch showed more leadership to businesses throughout the world than he did to GE where his contribution was at least as much managerial as leadership. This claim isn't obviously credible, even if you're not a Jack Welch fan.

Consider an analogy where this point is easier to see. Suppose you're on the beach with your 3 small children. There are a dozen other families on the beach. As the day gets hotter, you buy your children an ice cream cone. Many other parents soon follow your example. You made a unilateral decision to buy ice cream cones so this doesn't count as leadership to your children, but your example to other families showed leadership to them.

So, to the extent that Jack Welch made unilateral decisions to introduce his revolutionary ideas, he made managerial decisions. But, he was clearly a pioneer relative to many other enterprises across the globe at the time so his example showed leadership to them. This is because his actions influenced them to follow his example. He could not dictate anything to them as he could at GE.

This is counterintuitive because we normally think of those in charge as showing leadership if they make sound strategic decisions. I narrow the focus of leadership in two ways. by saying that it pertains only to the promotion of new directions, hence having nothing to do with managing people or implementation. Secondly, not being a role, it can only influence people informally. This means that making decisions *for* a group is never leadership but actually a management activity.

But there is a different sense in which Jack Welch could be seen as a leader at GE. He was looked up to, admired, feared, respected. He was courageous, strong, decisive and determined. He was the stereotype of the traditional leader. Our hard-wired tendency to form ourselves into hierarchies, along with most of the rest of the animal kingdom, makes this a biologically archaic form of leadership. It's also psychologically primitive because our ideal of a good leader is founded on our ideal of a good father – one we can look up to and who takes care of us. A bad father is one who punishes and controls us.

This dichotomy partly explains our irrationally negative attitude toward management. What is normally called followership is a combination of hero worship and submission. We disempower ourselves by putting all our faith in one person to give us answers, solve our problems and soothe our anxieties. The rage we feel toward failed leaders is in direct proportion to our expectations of them. We may not be able to change our hard-wired tendencies but we can reframe how we view traditional leaders. We can call them executives instead and avoid the term "leader" as much as possible, striving to see only the championing of new directions as leadership.

There is no denying that Jack Welch played a central role

in transforming General Electric. But was he a leader or mainly a manager? According to Noel Tichy, Welch regarded himself as a manager in his early days. Midway through the eighties Welch is described by Tichy as wanting GE executives to become leaders not managers. In large part, this switch seems to imply becoming coaches and facilitators rather than autocratic controllers.[2]

Tichy tells us that "Management is fine as far as it goes, but leadership is the way to win. GE has created an organization designed to demand leadership from every one of its members."[3] Managers were given so much to do that they had to empower people. So, "Leaders' success depends on the ability to assemble and motivate teams of people who can accomplish tasks by themselves".[4]

But surely this isn't leadership if the goal is just to empower people to execute set directions independently. In fact, it's merely a change in management style – from a controlling, autocratic one to a style based on motivation and empowerment. But if Welch was a manager both before and after his style change, how was he a leader?

Without question Welch was a powerful traditional or paternal leader because of his commanding presence and autocratic, iron-fisted rule over GE. In the early days, he used the incredible force of his personality to muscle his way to the top of the hierarchy. (I explore what it means to be a paternal leader in the next chapter.) When in power, Jack Welch seems to have tolerated no opposition. His decisions were law. Employees feared him as much as respected and admired him.

Still, Welch's success in getting things done with amazing speed won the admiration of executives both inside and outside GE. This means that he had a leadership impact on thousands of people around the world through his example. This is true despite the fact that any decisions he made were managerial acts rather than leadership as here conceived.

Welch initiated several ideas in GE that were copied everywhere – being 1 or 2 in a market, six sigma quality, workout.

Even if these initiatives were managerial decisions, they provided leadership to executives in other organizations. A forum for generating solutions to problems such as workout could be seen as an example of process leadership. But this would only be the case if employees were persuaded rather than ordered to get involved in it.

You could also see workout as encouraging leadership in employees, but in GE it doesn't seem to have been conceived this way. Workout sessions ended with employees presenting proposals to their managers for instant decisions. To see this as upward leadership, it needs to be reframed as such, not just seen as old fashioned suggestion-box material for the "real leaders" to mull over.

What about Welch's vision? In Tichy's words, Welch defined his vision in "a few simple ideas: integrated diversity, boundarylessness, global leadership, the business engine."[5] Even if he decided on his vision unilaterally, championing it throughout GE shows leadership.

In short, Jack Welch provided his clearest leadership by example (especially to other firms) and by promoting a vision within GE. He was also a leader in a paternal sense.

Concluding comments

The point of this chapter has been to distribute the activities of executives across a range of roles to show the multiple ways in which they can add value. The underlying motivation for this chapter, however, is to throw into sharp relief what counts as leadership and what doesn't. I have done this by distributing what is normally seen as leadership across a range of other functions that do not amount to leadership except in the trivial sense that they're displayed by people in formal positions. In this chapter, I referred to Jack Welch as a traditional or paternal leader because I think we need to account for our deep-seated desire to look up to and depend on such people. I turn to this issue in greater depth in the next chapter.

Tom Bower's questions and my replies

Tom asked

> "I can see myself in several of your executive functions, but why precisely these ones?"

"You could cut the cake up another way or in a different number of pieces, Tom. I had three aims here: first, to show that leadership is only one of the things executives get up to. Second, I wanted to show that executives spend a lot of time *doing*, hence neither managing nor leading. The point is to help executives see how they're investing their time so they can make better, emotionally intelligent decisions about how to allocate their time. Third, by showing executives such a wide range of ways they can add value, this account might reduce their anxiety over having to give up some of the leadership stage."

"Okay, you're saying that these functions aren't cast in stone, just that there are lots of things we do that don't count as leadership."

"Yes, Tom, that's it. To get executives to buy my reframed story of leadership and start fostering it more actively in others, I need to make them see the vital importance of their other activities. Management is at least as critical as leadership. Without good management, there would be no stimulating environment in which leadership could emerge or flourish. Managers are like gardeners. With no nurturing, their gardens would become weeds."

"I like the idea of seeing myself as an investor except that it sounds a bit hands-off. I'm much more involved in running things than an investor."

"No problem but when you get involved you might be operating as a Catalyst, Coach or wearing one of the Doing hats. It might help to think of investors as customers; they're quite similar. Both only buy what they think will give them good value. There might be times when you need to be the world's most demanding customer or investor to get what you want out of your organization (your internal suppliers). Calling those shots is a key part of your role and not one you should ignore just because we relabel it as something other than leadership."

"Fine, but I'm not sure I buy your take on Jack Welch though. He's widely admired and for good reason."

"I'm not denying his worthiness of admiration, Tom. I've stressed the importance of management. We just need to start admiring managers as much as we do leaders. But my other reason for talking about Jack Welch here is to set the stage for my critique in the next chapter of what I call paternal or primitive leadership."

CHAPTER 5

The End of Primitive Leadership

LEADERS ARE NORMALLY seen as those people who have what it takes to get to the top. Even if we agree that leadership isn't a position, we still cling to the idea that leaders take charge, rise to the occasion and direct, organize or coordinate our efforts toward a goal. Leaders who do not take charge but rather facilitate the finding of direction in others are rightly seen as "paradoxical" because they "lead by not leading."[1]

This chapter digs into our deep-set need for traditional leaders, our pursuit of hierarchy, status and power. We can't change our biology or ditch primitive psychological needs but we can stop calling bosses leaders. Why not say they're chief executives or simply chiefs instead? But names are only on the surface. The real aim of this chapter is to heighten awareness of how disempowering it is to allow leadership to be monopolized by those with the power to dominate us. Regardless of label, we need to expand our thinking to include other types of leadership.

Leadership as sitting on top of the pile

In a study of political leadership, *King of the Mountain*, Arnold M. Ludwig claims that "all the usual reasons aspiring rulers give for seeking high office are simply rationalizations by them to do what they are socially and biologically driven to do."[2] Chief executives might have grand visions to build successful businesses that become number one in a market, but they're also driven by basic biological urges to dominate others for all the usual benefits that propel other (especially male) animals. Ludwig suggests that we can't avoid this archaic pattern: "The need for a single leader to be head of a social unit seems biologically and psychologically rooted in our being. It's part of the genetic blueprint that governs our lives. The drive to be the alpha male provides the basic impetus for the dominance hierarchy, which ... seems to govern most social interactions among higher primates."[3]

In *Managing the Human Animal*, Nigel Nicholson applies evolutionary psychology to leadership which he defines as "the positions of highest authority within a social group."[4] Nicholson argues that "Dominance is a biological universal for all social mammals."[5] Referring to how we learn about dominance, Nicholson states: "The vocabulary of dominance is universal – an upright stance, decisive gestures, strong voice, and an unflinching gaze."[6] So there is little chance of becoming a leader if you do not have the personal power to dominate others. As Nicholson explains: "As we enter the age of biology and the decoding of the human genome, it's time to return to the idea that some people are simply born with potentialities for leadership."[7]

In *The Managerial Mystique*, well before the evolutionary psychology craze, Abraham Zaleznik wrote "In study after study of group formations ... leaders and followers align themselves into a remarkably predictable relationship with few at the top and many at the bottom of the power pyramid."[8] He added that "When hierarchy is absent, social relations are subject to the pains of anxiety."[9] People in a group struggle to establish their status, feeling anxious until they know who to turn to for the resolution of disputes and the distribution of rewards. Anyone who advocates the dismantling of hierarchy is called a utopian by Zaleznik, an unrealistic dreamer who ignores the basic facts of human nature. This pessimism shows what a challenge it is to dismantle or even minimize hierarchy. Flatter structures mean little, if power differences between top and bottom are as great as ever.

> It's as easy to be dependent, deferential, disempowered or subservient through three layers as ten.

While personal urges to climb the ladder are hidden behind good intentions, they can wreak havoc. Executives scheme to retain their grip on power by scuttling rivals, ousting potential enemies and postponing the development of successors. The result is an internal focus that can cripple an executive's ability to show genuine leadership. How much energy and time is wasted by pretenders to the throne clambering for the top themselves? Aspiring executives must offer something new, but they avoid challenging the status quo too strongly for fear of antagonizing their sponsors. This mindset can squash leadership motivation in the lower ranks. Competition for top slots is a win-lose game with many more losers than winners.

For early humans and lower animals, superior brute strength propelled the ascent. Today the force of personality is the winning formula, a more subtle display of animal magnetism and strength than a physical attack on rivals. We submit to this primitive power either out of admiration bordering on hero worship, indifference or fear. Whatever the reason, we disempower ourselves by expecting all leadership to emanate from the top.

Paternalism and leadership

Compare leaders and managers with good and bad fathers. A good father entertains, inspires, protects and does great things – our hero. Bad fathers tell us what to do, discipline, punish and control us. They make us do things we do not want to do and stop us doing what we like doing. The popular view of leadership is totally *paternalistic*.

A paternal leader is the group's father substitute. A good father makes us feel good about pouring so much time and energy into our work. We acknowledge his right to play the heavy, still regarding him as a good father (leader) so long as he isn't too heavy too often. If the balance is wrong and the predominant style is bullying or disciplinarian, then he is a bad father, a manager, not a real leader.

Paternal leaders play on this psychology by making us feel guilty when we're bad and patting us on the head when we're good. This isn't their fault. We collude by demanding that our managers be good fathers (leaders).

How do you feel about your boss?

We have a range of attitudes toward our bosses, thanks in part to our feelings about authority. As with other animal hierarchies, some defy authority, seeing themselves as successors at the top of the pile. Others lack the confidence or are short of the raw power to push incumbents aside. At our most fearful we expect leaders to protect us, to allay our anxieties and fears. We fear change not so much because of the change itself, but because of how it might disrupt our relationship to our hero or protector.

Aspiring leaders scheme to displace their superiors without undermining the system. They collude in preserving hierarchy so there is always a ladder to climb. In between these two extremes are those who are neither fearful nor ambitious, but who simply admire and follow their heroes. Most employees, in one way or another, preserve this myth about leadership. When leaders fail, their challengers are delighted and are quick to scorn them to elevate themselves. Hero-worshippers are disillusioned, while the fearful are paralyzed by anxiety. All unite in finger-pointing. Having someone to blame relieves us of pressure to take responsibility for our own fears and failings.

Parent-child or adult-adult relationships?

Transactional analysis sheds light on this drama by sharply contrasting adult and parent-child relationships. Paternal leaders behave like fathers and we see them that way, good or bad. This pushes us to feel and behave like children and we fall along a continuum ranging from rebellion to submission. Relating in a parent-child way is to talk down to people rather than on an adult, equal basis. A benevolent parent is overly sympathetic and nurturing, which creates a child-like dependency as surely as what the critical parent achieves through scolding. Whenever you're critical, demanding or highly sympathetic, you're in parent mode.

We can fall into the pattern of parent-child interactions without trying. If you're berating a colleague, just as your parents once did to you, then you're behaving like a parent. Similarly, if you're comforting someone in an overly condescending or patronizing way, then your manner is just as parental. An adult-adult relationship is one of mutual respect. Neither side is one down or one up. Conversely, if you feel a childish level of fear or respect for your boss, then you're relating to him or her as your parent. A manager could well nudge you down this road, but it might actually be *your* needs driving him or her to relate to you this way. It's a two-way street. Both parties must willingly play the game for a paternalistic relationship to develop and persist. Where the needs of both parties are thus served, it's a difficult habit to break.

Do you need to see yourself as an all-powerful parent figure to feel confident? Those in the child role might be too fearful to act independently. They might find it too difficult to face the challenges of life or work without paternal support. Often we slip into this way of relating because others relate to us this way. If we see someone throwing a temper tantrum and we become overly comforting or chastising, then we've been sucked into the parent role without trying. Or, if someone who is angry with us adopts a critical tone in unloading their anger, it's easy to fall into childlike feelings of remorse, guilt, anger or hurt.

Add formal authority to the mix and paternalism is harder to avoid. Bosses, like fathers, have megawatts of power over us. They have the authority (the right) to discipline us, tell us what to do, what not to do and, ultimately, to fire us. Both sides must work hard to achieve an adult-adult relationship, assuming it's desired by both players. Some managers like their job for the parental gratification it provides. Having power over, or responsibility for, others can be as satisfying as anything actually achieved through people. Similarly, some employees need a strong boss to avoid feeling nervous and alone.

> The paternal model of leadership is a colossal waste of human energy in a complex, competitive world where all employees must be fully functioning adults able to make independent, confident decisions.

Paternalism is also counterproductive because so much energy is diverted into sustaining the system. Like the guy said: "We have our eyes on the boss and our asses to the customer." Some plot his downfall while the rest are seeking his approval or protection.

Are you a paternal leader?

To be a paternal leader, you do not have to see yourself explicitly as a father figure. The paternal mindset is so ingrained as to be off our radar screens. Many managers talk about "my people" as if referring to their family. Managers expect more loyalty and respect from their direct reports than from other business associates. If you disagree, ask yourself how you feel about those who leave to join another employer. Why should you expect more loyalty from someone who reports to you than you do from a colleague? If you genuinely relate to your subordinates on an adult-adult basis, you could view them as partners instead of implicitly as your children.

Today's oft heard cry for more and better leadership is, in fact, not just an objective desire for clearer direction, but a cry for protection from the anxiety of rising chaos. As rapid change and complexity escalate, our fears and anxieties rise in hot pursuit, driving us to demand more and better leaders (fathers). And the closer our anxiety gets to crisis levels, the more we disempower ourselves and hope that some good father will save us.

Are you a genuine or paternal leader/manager?

Paternal	Non-paternal
Do you ...?	Or do you ...?
• prefer routine operations	• champion change
• focus mainly internally	• focus mainly externally
• like status	• play down status
• enjoy deference	• discourage deference
• like exercising authority	• foster decision making
• insist on having final word	• let others decide
• relish trappings of office	• avoid office trappings
• preserve hierarchy	• break down hierarchy
• be protective	• empower extensively
• demand loyalty	• win respect
• see self as irreplaceable	• admire others' strengths
• hog the limelight	• listen supportively
• make unilateral decisions	• sell decisions to other
• flip from angry to nice	• remain even-tempered

Which side of the fence are you on? Does your culture push you to the paternal side by loading enormous pressure on you to deliver? If you get too involved in detail or hog the psychological ownership for everything, you might feel overly important and see your team as just your support service rather than as an equal partner. Feeling too strongly the weight of responsibility is a recipe for paternalism.

How can you be less paternalistic?

The less paternalistic you are, the more confidently your team will challenge you. If they do not automatically defer to your wisdom, then you must work harder to convince them to change direction, showing genuine leadership. They then see your influence as appealing to their reason or adult emotions rather than just an exercise of your parental authority. They feel they have the right to think for themselves and question the benefits of the direction you advocate. Conversely, if you're paternalistic, then even your genuine leadership attempts will not be separable in practice from paternalistic leadership. You could well strive to sell change, but because you're seen as the boss, your team defers rather than being genuinely persuaded. Leadership is in the eye of the beholder.

If your team is in deferential mode, they might grumble about change, but see it as your right to make even questionable decisions. For example, in a team meeting, you make a strong case for a change in direction, striving to influence (lead) rather than impose. Some team members are won over by the strength of your arguments, but others acquiesce simply because they see it as your job to make such decisions. Here, genuine leadership is only shown to those won over by the power of your business case. Others are not led because they're programmed to see you as the boss. Overcoming this compulsion isn't easy.

"What does it matter?' you object, as long as the change is smoothly implemented. It matters because every time you force a change through, no matter how docile the resistance, you disempower everyone who defers to you. This pattern reinforces paternal relationships and undermines any effort you have made to lift people to a more adult level without fear to challenge you.

> Disempowered employees don't use their brains fully because they see *thinking* as the boss's job and *doing* as theirs. They abdicate responsibility because the boss snatches it away. This is costly because the investment in people yields a severely limited payback. The boss is then caught in the vicious circle of having to do all the thinking because no one else will. And no one else will because the boss has turned them off.

The moral of this story is that no paternal leader can ever display genuine leadership no matter how correct the proposed change of direction might be. Visualize yourself as Martin Luther King or any other outsider leader with no formal authority. Now you have to *enlist* support solely through the strength of your influencing skills. This is genuine leadership. To show real leadership, engineer your culture so that only genuine influence attempts gain the acceptance of followers.

If the thought of disempowering yourself is hard to swallow, remember anything you've already done to empower employees entails some disempowerment for yourself. If you're granting employees the right to make some decisions that you once made, you're letting go of the power to make those decisions yourself. The key, therefore, is to take empowerment a step further so employees genuinely feel confident to provide leadership to you sometimes – to strive to sell you new ideas and to challenge your proposals.

Traditional leadership up in smoke

Traditional leadership is anchored in our hardware and software. Whatever we call the person in charge, we insist on having one person to look up to, someone we can trust to look after us and point us in the right direction. Even if we agree to stop calling this leadership, we could still yearn for the support that such figures offer. Doubtless some wisdom comes with long experience, which Daniel Goleman repackaged as emotional intelligence. But can we not seek the support of mentors without calling them leaders? When we lack confidence, we like direction from those who have it. Decisive people are admired by the indecisive. Also, those who can dominate will continue to do so for the usual psychological or material benefits.

Referring to those in charge as leaders will persist out of habit, just as we continued to call planets and stars heavenly bodies long after they were shown to be nothing but earthly dirt and rock. Galileo enraged people when his telescope revealed blemishes on the moon and sun because heavenly bodies could not have any imperfections. Changing how we label executives is just as gut-wrenching.

To fully empower employees we need to build their confidence to assert themselves and challenge the status quo, not an easy task unless we can rid ourselves of primitive leadership. Without denying our unalterable biology and psychological needs, we need to reclassify the process of getting people to work productively as a management activity and stop calling it leadership.

Conclusions on primitive leadership

Leadership rebuilt on the power to promote new ideas isn't hierarchical or paternal but it still has a biological basis. The drive to challenge authority, rebel, or differentiate yourself is unlearned. Unlike conventional leadership, which is based on the drive to dominate, all employees want to stand out, to make their mark, especially in their youth. This means that leadership is open to the many, not just the few with the urge to dominate.

Either way, the core of leadership is an unlearned trait or

disposition, something that can be fostered not developed. What this implies for the leadership development industry is explained in the next chapter.

Tom Bower's questions and my replies

"Let me get this straight," Tom Bower demanded, "It sounds like you're saying it's OK for me to be a sort of fatherly container for people's anxiety if that's what they really need from me, but the better I am in meeting those needs, the harder it is for me to show genuine leadership. This feels like a no-win place to be."

"That's right, Tom. The more they see you as a parent, the more they see it as your right to call the shots, to be a manager, not a leader."

"Actually, that's not my problem. My HR director is the nurturing type. People see me as the nasty one who takes a hard line, but you're going to tell me that this isn't showing leadership either, right?"

"You shouldn't expect to excel in all the executive roles. This is why you should be strategic about matching your strengths with your business's needs. How often do you need to show genuine leadership? What percentage of your time and effort should be devoted to supporting others, being a coach, catalyst, steward or investor?"

"I see what you mean. If I apply the 80-20 rule, our industry is more about great execution than constantly reinventing ourselves. Still there are times when I want people to change and for them to own it. Are you saying that I can't get people to own a new direction because my pushing it will make them see me through parental lenses and just acquiesce in my right to decide?"

"That's a great question, Tom. It really goes to the heart of what I'm banging on about. If you want others to own a decision to do something different, you have to involve them in the thinking behind what direction to pursue. Asking them open, supportive questions is what the CEOs in Jim Collins's good to great companies did. My point is that this is managerial activity. If you're not championing the new yourself, then you're wearing a managerial hat, operating as a coach or catalyst, not showing leadership.'

"So, the bottom line is I could be totally successful while hardly ever showing any real leadership as you define it. I hope you realize that this is really blowing my mind. You're not saying it's impossible for a CEO to show leadership but it may not often be necessary."

"Correct. CEOs in the Jim Collins *Good to Great* story are facilitators, not leaders at all. Their success lies in stimulating genuine leadership in everyone else."

"But what am I doing when I promote a new vision around our place?"

"It's a mixture. If you involve people in developing your vision, you're a facilitator, a manager. But your repeated affirmation of the vision, after it's agreed, will be seen as real leadership by many, even if some see it as your decision."

"Okay, that feels better. So I can show some leadership when I promote a new vision, but what you're saying is that I'm fussing about whether I'm seen as a leader when that's not even important. I'm beginning to see the light but it'll take me some time yet to get my head around it."

"But can you see benefits for you in this way of thinking?"

"Yes, definitely. I can put less pressure on myself to be all things to all people and just do what I do best. By cultivating leadership throughout the business, we should be better able to motivate and retain good people."

"Not to mention unleashing a flood of good ideas."

CHAPTER 6

Foster Leadership, Develop Executives

NEARLY EVERYONE SEES leadership as a set of skills that anyone can develop. But this is only credible if we lump leadership and management together or define leadership as getting things done through people. But once we slice away the managerial bits, we have a concept of leadership that isn't so clearly a set of learnable skills.

No doubt, management is a set of skills that can be learned: how to organize, coordinate and direct the efforts of others, how to motivate and develop people.

If the core of leadership can't be developed, are the many doomed to followership? No, as we noted in Chapter Three, if everyone can show leadership now, does it matter if it can't be learned? Traditional leadership is much more exclusive for being hierarchical – there is only so much room at the top. The courage to show leadership seen as a free-floating guerrilla activity is a matter of degree. Everyone can show some leadership. And, as already noted, everyone's courage fluctuates, rising with suitable provocation on the spur of the moment. So, even the most reticent can be provoked to take a stand on something at some point in their lives.

The fate of conventional leadership development programs isn't so rosy: they develop rounded executives or managers, not leaders. People show leadership before obtaining a responsible position. Getting promoted transforms leaders into managers. It doesn't make leaders out of non-leaders. In this chapter I look at what can and can't be developed. Then I review the implications of this thinking for conventional leadership development before turning to the question of how to foster leadership.

What can be developed?

First of all, what does it take to lead people?

If leadership is promoting new directions, not managing people, you need three things:

1. Something worth saying
2. The courage to say it.
3. Influencing skills

Which of these factors can you develop? The first and third are likely candidates. You learn about some field in life or work, find something to get excited about, and you take a stand. Being creative helps, but you might be an early adopter of new ideas and show leadership by promoting adopted ideas to others. Or, someone might show leadership to you and you then do the same with others.

Influencing skills can also be shaped. You can learn techniques for influencing people even though it isn't easy to develop the oratory of a Martin Luther King if you're a shy, soft spoken introvert. There is a limit to how much you can shift your basic influencing style.

Still, influencing skills are more learnable than courage. Like creativity, courage is a natural trait we all have in varying degrees. You can improve your creativity marginally by learning creative thinking tricks but, more importantly, it can be bolstered by the right environment and stimulation from others. Blocks to creativity can be removed – fear of failure, lack of exposure to creative others, noise and distractions.

Similarly for courage: we can foster it by removing blocks, the biggest one being fear. Why are people afraid to take a stand on a new product, service or principle? If we set aside the fear of death that plagues front-line military personnel, here are some candidates:

- Fear of rejection and ridicule by colleagues.
- Fear of losing your job or being sidelined.
- Fear of making a mistake, being wrong.

Some fear-reducing tips

- Test your idea out on a neutral pilot group.
- Work toward the main idea with small steps or hints.
- Ask questions to draw your idea out of others.
- Form alliances with more courageous colleagues.
- Have lots of friends so you can afford to lose a few.
- Be diplomatic, especially when challenging your boss.
- Try your idea out, if possible, to avoid a mistake.
- Develop a fall-back plan if you do make a mistake.
- Network so you have other career options.
- Develop your nerve by first promoting safer ideas.
- Find a supportive mentor.

No doubt you can think of other ways to lift your courage a notch, but none of them amounts to learning a new skill.

Highly courageous people do not get that way through learning or study. Like creative people, some are naturally more courageous than others while some are more risk averse, cautious or shy. Early upbringing helps to shape people at both ends of the spectrum but neither creativity nor courage are qualities you can learn on a leadership development program.

If courage is central to leadership and can't be developed, then what is the leadership development industry doing?

Conventional leadership development programs

So-called leadership development programs cover more management skills than genuine leadership. At best they prepare people for broader, more responsible roles. At worst they inhibit potential leaders by rounding off their rebellious edges, as when you convert your best sales people or engineers into poor managers.

The main emphasis of conventional programs is how to manage a team – how to coach, motivate and develop "your people", how to delegate and communicate. This is all management development, nothing to do with leadership.

Vision is a leadership topic, but often only a small part of the total training event. Everything to do with "leadership style" is about management style. All the old stuff about how to delegate – when, what, and to whom, pertains to management not leadership. How to make decisions, whether to be directive or participative, is also a management style issue, again nothing to do with leadership. Managers make decisions about what tasks to do next and how to do them efficiently. Leaders influence people to change direction.

Values, trust, integrity, character and emotional intelligence are critical for rounded senior executives because of their responsibilities for people, money and other organizational resources but none of this impacts the meaning of leadership. Showing leadership only requires such factors for influencing people situationally. If it's possible to show leadership without these traits, then it can't be defined by reference to them.

Kouzes and Posner's view of leadership development is popular. They advise aspiring leaders to look inside themselves. In a section of *The Leadership Challenge*, called "Look in the mirror" they state: "Clarification of personal values begins with becoming more self-aware."[1] This advice surely helps people prepare for responsible roles. But thought leadership is an occasional act, not a role, hence not a set of responsibilities. Would-be thought leaders need to immerse themselves in a relevant technology, not indulge in navel gazing. They often block out their surroundings, forgetting to eat, wash and sleep. Taking time out to mull over their personal values is a distraction they wouldn't swallow.

Developing managers and rounded executives

Reframing leadership development as executive development isn't enough. A critical addition is to improve the image of management so it's seen as positively as it is in sports. Professional golfers have managers who provide a service to their clients with no power to order them around. Also, we need management heroes to serve as role models for aspiring executives like those Jim Collins celebrates in *Good to Great* who built their businesses by being facilitative, not by championing their own visions.

Successful sports coaches are managers with excellent motivational skills. Executives need to shift the basis of their identity and develop a new source of self-worth. It isn't about never showing leadership, but of recognizing other, non-leadership ways of adding value and the need to share the leadership limelight with all employees.

Executives also need to learn to be more receptive to upward challenges. The Chief executives that Jim Collins celebrates had plenty of emotional strength, although he calls it unassuming modesty. But executives get to the top by promoting their own ideas, scoring a lot of goals. To stop doing what got them to the top is a huge emotional challenge. It's hard enough for sports coaches to leave the playing field. For them, age forces the issue, but executives are playing coaches. They have to get the balance right, to stop their drive to score goals from getting in the way of coaching younger players.

> Coping with upward challenges means learning to respond less defensively, to take criticism constructively, control anger and maintain self esteem.

Your example and Bill Gates

If your identity is wrapped up in the work itself, you could make a clean break of it as Bill Gates did when he passed the Chief executive role to Steve Ballmer. When Gates became Chairman of the Board, he took the title "Chief Software Architect," making it clear to Microsoft employees that he wanted to show leadership in the content of the business. His identity and strongest skills are bound up with the content of the business. Being a general manager was perhaps not fully satisfying to him.

Still, even in the role of Chief Software Architect, Gates can carry out some executive functions (coaching and facilitating) in addition to showing content leadership through a new product vision or specific software ideas. In a March, 2005 Business Week article, Gates offered some visionary leadership: "I believe that computing will change our lives more in the next 10 years than it has in the past quarter-century – and that the PC, in all its forms, will be the centerpiece of this new wave of innovation."[3]

In an early 2005 conference, he was clear about his role. Speaking of the 5 facets of Microsoft's strategy, Gates told his audience "And so it's really my role to make sure that we're delivering on each of these five areas …".[4] This effort is managerial as it involves execution of set targets, facilitation, coaching and staff motivation. So, Gates offers content leadership and some managerial facilitation. He is clear about how he can add value by making best use of his strengths and interests.

An executive's desire to focus on technology shows the

need for career options that don't force everyone onto the managerial ladder. Think of the pioneering heart transplant surgeon Cristiaan Barnard who enjoyed a successful career and global thought leadership status with no managerial accolades. Many doctors and other knowledge workers are valued for their content contributions without being managers. Executive development programs should help participants identify their primary drivers and strengths so they can shape their careers accordingly. The one-size-fits-all approach wastefully forces all with ambition to fit a uniform, corporate-wide competency profile.

Another essential addition to executive development programs is the skill of fostering leadership in others where leadership is properly reframed. The real challenge here is the emotional adjustment, moving from seeing oneself as a leader to being happy as a manager.

Finally, executives need to develop a new understanding of how they can show leadership. They can show as much thought leadership as non-managerial employees but doing so means immersion in products and processes to develop or spot new ideas to promote. This requires more time with customers, analysing markets and picking the brains of leading edge thinkers in their markets. Executive leadership can take the form of a broad vision of the future or of ideas for specific products, businesses or markets. Their development efforts, however, must highlight the trade-offs that intense involvement in the content of the business demands relative to other responsibilities. Other functions are neglected if they're not assigned to colleagues.

Conclusions on conventional training programs

Developing managers is now more important than ever. Their role is arguably more critical than leaders. They have the dual responsibility of making things happen well enough to turn a profit and to foster leadership in others through their individual support and by cultivating a stimulating culture. This is enough to be heroic without showing leadership too. It's time for a total rethink of executive development programs.

Fostering Leadership

In this section, I outline steps for fostering leadership in all employees. I also discuss the implications of leadership reframed for career management, how fostering bottom-up leadership encourages employees to be more proactive in managing their careers.

Fostering leadership requires a supportive culture, one that stimulates people to be courageous and challenge the status quo, thereby showing leadership. Unfortunately, many cultures dampen the rebellious spirit by advising caution. The following widely deployed mantras stifle risk-taking, being unconventional and taking a controversial line:

- Think of your impact before challenging people.
- Be balanced; examine the implications of your ideas.
- Consider customer and shareholder sensitivities.
- Be sure to take people with you, involve others, win their support.
- Deliver your results this quarter and every quarter.
- Drive down costs, improve service to customers.
- Get things right first time.
- Do not reinvent the wheel.
- Do not make a mistake or take undue risks.
- Show respect for your elders.
- Be a team player.
- Coach and develop people, set an example.
- Think deeply about the sort of person you are before speaking up.
- Be emotionally intelligent (mature).

How to support bottom-up leadership

- Reward iconoclastic actions and promoting new ideas.
- Stop punishing mistakes and risk-taking.
- Celebrate challenging upward.
- Set innovation targets.
- Get prospective leaders close to pertinent markets, customers and competitors – keep them at the sharp edge of product development.
- Minimize hierarchy, status and positional power.
- Celebrate management in addition to leadership.
- Implement more idea-sharing communication channels.
- Create more flexible roles to discourage saying "That's not my job," thereby creating a more entrepreneurial attitude that helps employees see the whole organization as a potential market for their ideas.
- Eliminate fear – whatever intimidates employees.
- Foster diversity: stop saying "you're not a team player."

Offer support to managers

- Show them the meaning and importance of their responsibilities.
- Show how they can encourage leadership in others.
- Explain how they can show leadership as well.
- Help them adjust to more challenging employees, to be less defensive, to build a new identity for themselves.
- Explain how they can best add value.
- Provide training on active listening and facilitation – how to coach and draw solutions out of others.
- Play down the excessive individualism that rewards executives for scoring all the goals themselves.
- Celebrate heroic managers and leaders not heroic doers.

Fostering leadership in all

- Help employees discover their strongest preferences.
- Identify role-models for them – those with a spirit of adventure strong enough to challenge upwards.
- Tell stories of those who show thought leadership.
- Clarify career options – how employees can advance by different routes – those that major on management competence and those that show promise of leadership.
- Enable those with leadership potential to advance their careers as professionals or sole contributors.
- Expose creative types to others for cross-fertilization and a sense of not being an outcast or lone wolf.
- Ensure that initial steps to generate new directions are recognized and encouraged to build confidence.
- Avoid shooting people down when their ideas seem impractical. Ask supportive questions to help them build on their initial thoughts.
- Ensure they understand the nature of real leadership, especially that it isn't about having a position of power over a team, that it can be directed up and sideways and that they can start NOW.
- Offer training on influencing skills.
- Help employees see this culture change as a liberating opportunity, a chance to show their initiative and to promote their own careers rather than acquiescing in the usual disempowered mindset of merely waiting for the powers-that-be to notice them.

Influencing skills for bottom-up leaders

We've discussed two of the factors required to show leadership: having something to say and the courage to say it. This leaves influencing skills as the only leadership element that can be developed. Enough has been said about influencing skills elsewhere so I confine myself to a few comments that bear on bottom-up leadership.

The most powerful influencing tactic is to demonstrate how your idea works – assuming it's the sort of thing that can be demonstrated. Many bottom-up leadership initiatives are only successful because the new ideas were demonstrated, as when web pioneers at IBM showed their superiors how the web worked as discussed in Gary Hamel's *Leading the Revolution*,[5] an excellent documentation of thought leadership although he doesn't develop this concept. This works well enough with products that can be released on a small scale, trial basis, but not so well with a new aircraft design where you have to make a fully convincing case without the support of customer feedback or experiment.

Influencing upward in a traditional culture can be a challenge where managers expect deference from subordinates. Some managers like to think they have the answers. They fly into a rage if you tell them they're wrong. A subtle approach, however, might make your proposal seem like a mutual decision or even their idea.

A useful technique, no matter what your personality type, is to ask people to list what they see as the benefits of your proposal both for them and the organization. When people resist an idea they focus on negative features hence miss the benefits. It also helps to ask them what would need to be the case for them to buy your idea. Then you might show them how your proposal meets their criteria.

Often, the obvious approach of stating arguments for your proposal is resisted simply because you're *telling* people – this is aggressive no matter what your tone of voice because it's one-way communication. Asking questions about your target audience's needs or ideas generates dialogue, a more fruitful basis for progress than a sermon, no matter how powerfully or passionately delivered it might be.

Anyone with children knows how independent they are from a very young age. They insist on feeding themselves, throwing a temper tantrum if you try to do things for them. As adults we overly rely on making a sales pitch to influence people, but this approach amounts to doing their thinking for them.

> Selling people ideas is resisted because it's doing their thinking for them.

Being sold to is resented on some level. So you have to be ultra inspiring or convincing to get over this hurdle. Better to avoid it by drawing ideas out of people so they feel involved in the decision. But, you ask, isn't this facilitation rather than leadership? Yes, if you have no view to promote yourself. But a deft combination of facilitation and presenting your own ideas still allows you to show leadership. *In this case, facilitation is an influencing style* rather than a means of generating good ideas from scratch. Asking facilitative questions is then a way of drawing people toward your conclusions, a subtle influencing tactic, not a brainstorming one.

Upward influence is more likely to succeed if it's subtle, especially in a culture of strong egos. An aggressive frontal attack can succeed, but I only highlighted this approach to make the point that leadership can be shown by these means. I never meant to suggest that such an influencing style is the best one.

The new team leadership

Team members can show leadership in two ways. Within their team they provide occasional leadership contributions. In addition, if the team as a whole generates powerful new directions for the rest of the organization, then the team has shown leadership to the broader organization. This idea isn't widely recognized because we traditionally associate leadership with the actions of a single person. But just as we have league leading teams in sports and market leading businesses, there's no reason why we shouldn't say that teams provide leadership. Because we no longer say leadership has to emanate from an individual, we can make sense of the idea that a team can lead other teams or a whole organization.

There is another way for individuals to help their teams show leadership. Even if their contributions are mainly managerial – active listening, facilitating, asking questions, resolving conflict and supporting others, they can help the team develop leadership ideas that could generate new directions for the organization as a whole. Hence they help their team show leadership to the organization without actually showing any leadership personally.

> Now, leadership can be fostered through teams without placing all the emphasis on individuals, a doubly empowering result. Even those individuals whose strongest skills are facilitative can still contribute to leading the organization by helping their teams come up with new ideas to promote, as a team.

Talent and career management

Thought leadership should be integrated with career management for better engagement and talent retention.

It is wise to invest in the careers of key players. Special efforts are made to develop critical staff while all employees are supported in managing their own careers. A balance is struck between top-down initiatives and self-managed career efforts. But too many employees still overly rely on management to promote them. Career self-management can be reframed as a search for leadership opportunities where employees are encouraged to search for new ways of contributing to the business that generate career opportunities for themselves as a side benefit.

Overcoming the dependency mindset

Even the most empowered employees can feel it's up to management to tap them on the shoulders and offer them a new position. Career frustration is as much due to a felt powerlessness to influence their career progress as the actual lack of advancement itself. Because they see management as holding all the strings, frustration leads the more vocal to complain while the rest simmer in silent resentment. Possible outcomes include demotivation, negative attitudes, lowered productivity, passive resistance to change and premature departure for greener pastures.

Saddled with a dependency mindset, employees expect management to do all the work of figuring out where to place them. Both sides focus on existing slots, most of which tend to be filled at any given point in time. *The key problem is that employees make the mistake of focusing on their own needs – what the organisation can do for them rather than the other way around.* Turning this on its head, employees need to discover or create new roles for themselves by finding new ways of adding value to the business. This means showing leadership instead of acquiescing as pawns on a chessboard.

Career management and leadership opportunities

Employees who view themselves as self-employed business people provide services to internal customers. Colleagues are potential strategic partners. The key point of this reframing is the realization that no business in its right mind would hope to succeed by *complaining* to its customers for not buying its services! For career success, employees must focus on their customers' needs, not their own. The latter will take care of themselves when they help their customers succeed. Those most effective in managing their careers seek opportunities to show leadership. They work closely with the business and internal customers, aiming to discover new ways of adding value. They then champion the changes for the benefit of the business in the first instance and, secondly, to generate career opportunities for themselves.

The wrong approach is simply to ask managers if they have a job opening. Employees need to do the hard work of probing and networking to find out what prospective internal customers are trying to achieve and then think creatively about how they can add value to the customer's efforts, thereby selling themselves and perhaps generating a new role they might fill. It isn't a matter of either complaining or boasting but of jointly creating new services that customers really want to buy.

Management's role is to foster bottom-up leadership rather than be gatekeepers for a pool of existing slots. Otherwise, managers are seen as blockers rather than as enablers. Hence the frustration and disengagement brought about by a paternalistic culture – the corollary of dependency.

Digging for leadership opportunities

Organizations are full of leadership opportunities that may not be visible unless someone digs them out. The process requires employees to ask the right questions to foster creative brainstorming. It isn't a matter of having an idea in advance to propose but rather of initiating a business dialogue with prospective internal customers that has the potential to generate new insights and opportunities. The right questions, asked supportively, can help managers step back and see what they're doing with a fresh perspective.

Benefits for the organization

- More proactive, fully engaged, employees thinking laterally about how to contribute more by focusing on the business first, their own needs second.
- Employees with more positive attitudes gained through a feeling of control, rather than simply waiting for management to do something for them.
- Greater cross-functional team work as employees seek

to work more closely with key players rather than see them as competitors or obstacles.
- Better relationships with employees when they see managers as customers, not as overseers.
- More leadership from employees, less dependency.

In summary

This chapter covered two related topics – how to develop executives and how to foster leadership. The first is a traditional training activity supplemented by coaching, action learning and job assignments. Fostering leadership isn't individual development. It requires the right culture. People can be taught influencing skills, but they need to be helped to raise their confidence to challenge upward.

Executive development programs need to be reframed so they no longer pretend to develop leaders. They can be structured much as they have always been with some additional emphasis on what leadership really means and what executives must do to foster leadership in others. Helping executives switch their identity from leadership to management is the hard part, hence why management needs to be upgraded so executives see how they can still be heroes without having to label themselves as leaders.

Tom Bower's questions and my replies

"I feel I'm getting the message," Tom observed, "but it's going to take a while to sink in. I have a lot of ambitious, big hitters on my senior team, big egos I suppose, who like to see themselves as leaders. Getting them to switch their heads to seeing themselves as managers isn't going to be easy. Even if I felt it could be done, I would need to be totally convinced it was worth doing. This is what I'm going to have to think more about."

"What do you think would win them over, Tom?"

"I think you've got all the arguments and benefits laid out

clearly enough. I just think I need to go through them a few more times to make them my own. As you've said, they can still show leadership."

'Yes, the key is to show them how such a revolution in leadership thinking benefits them. Ultimately, their main ambition is to be successful. They recognize, I presume, that this means getting the best out of people. So, the thing to do is to convince them that reframing leadership along these lines will help them be even more successful because they'll be able to motivate and retain people much more effectively."

"True enough. But your idea that leadership can't be developed isn't going to go over in a big way."

"How do you think you might convince them, Tom?"

"Well, it's only courage that you're saying can't be developed. So I suppose it's not a great leap to say that courage needs to be fostered rather than trained into people. Once I get them to see that all the learnable stuff is really managerial, they might see the light."

"You're right to be cautious, though Tom. The changes I'm advocating are complex and emotionally charged. On the complexity side, you need to help them see how management can be upgraded at the same time as getting them to buy a very different slant on leadership. You won't get there overnight, but do you think it's worth the effort."

"Yes, I think so. We're in a hellish battle with competitors. We can't improve efficiency and service fast enough. We need to do something different. I agree that all the old hype about leadership hasn't really changed in the last 30 years and it's not working anymore. The world is too different now. If we base leadership on promoting the new, I think we've got a viable way forward."

Conclusions for Part One

The Myths of Leadership Revisited

I started Part One by sketching a form of leadership – outsider or thought leadership – that is clearly distinct from management. The simple reason is that such outsiders are not necessarily involved in implementing what they're promoting. This reduces to ashes the myth that leadership is a position of authority, that it gets things done by managing people and that it's a way of maximizing the performance of a team that reports to the person in charge.

If leadership is slimmed down to promoting new directions, then everything we associate with conventional leadership must be a management activity. This is hard to see if we remain handicapped by an obsolete, narrow conception of management where managers are seen as mechanistic controllers, merely transactional, who can only relate to people through economic exchange. With management reformulated as an empowering, transformational activity, I was then able to draw a sharp distinction between leadership and management.

By limiting leadership to promoting new directions, it becomes clear that the requirements for showing leadership are simply having something worth saying and the courage to say it. The latter factor makes leadership not a learnable skill set although you can sharpen your influencing skills. This means that leadership can only be fostered and that leadership development programs actually develop rounded executives not leaders.

Most critically, something is missing – our much respected boss, the person we look up to and expect to look after us when the going gets tough. This is why I had to attack paternal or primitive leadership. Regardless of whether we're stuck with this ancient emotional programming, we can at least stop calling such people leaders.

In Part Two – *More Myths To Torch*, I spell out the implications of this view of leadership for a range of other popular leadership ideas.

Part Two
MORE MYTHS TO TORCH

HERE I COVER IMPLICATIONS of my reformulated concept of leadership for various popular views such as the well known account served up in *The Leadership Challenge* by Jim Kouzes and Barry Posner. I also discuss servant leadership, the question of whether women might be better leaders than men, the place of character, emotional intelligence and relationships in leadership.

Comparing my view of leadership with popular accounts should make it clearer. If you had never seen or heard of elephants, it would not help much to tell you that elephants are large, grey mammals with long ears and noses. You would want to know how they differ from other mammals. Hence why it's useful to compare my concept of leadership with popular versions. I also discuss how leadership differs from selling, teaching and other forms of influence.

Finally, I conclude by showing how leadership thus reframed ties in with postmodern themes. The main idea here is that there are no longer any final authorities on anything, that we must think for ourselves. This is exactly what I'm saying when I argue that leadership is becoming dispersed throughout organizations instead of monopolized by those in managerial positions.

CHAPTER 7

Kouzes and Posner on Leadership

AN ADMIRED VIEW of leadership today is that of Kouzes and Posner as set out in *The Leadership Challenge*.[1]

The Leadership Challenge is an inspiring book. Kouzes and Posner provide stirring advice for getting extraordinary things done in organizations. But their book would be more accurately titled *The Executive Challenge* because the coverage is far too broad to be considered leadership. Focus, a core aspect of what it means to be strategic, is missing. As a consequence, we're offered a heavily burdened account of leadership because there is no place for management. Kouzes and Posner began their quest to understand leadership in the 1980s when everyone was trashing management. Hence why Tom Peters said in the foreword to their first edition of 1987 "... management as we know it isn't dead. But it darned well ought to be!"[2] This foreword isn't in their third edition of 2002, but Kouzes and Posner still don't mention management, not even to dismiss it. The result is that their view of leadership is far too broad, placing a colossal weight of ownership on executives.

Kouzes and Posner's fusing of leadership and management is evident in their journey metaphor: "In this book, and in all our discussions or leadership, we use the journey metaphor to express our understanding of leadership."[3] This means that leaders not only inspire people to undertake journeys, they do everything to facilitate reaching the destination as well. This is surely a mistake, one based on the old fashioned, entrenched belief that we should focus on the whole person in a role in charge of a group, formally or informally, to understand leadership.

As I argued in Chapter One, thought leadership doesn't even entail action, let alone a journey. Further, when a journey is required, the thought leader isn't necessarily the one to orchestrate getting to the destination. This implies that the meaning of leadership can't be based on the metaphor of a journey. Rejecting this image gives us the wedge to drive leadership and management apart. Once we make this move, we can then allot to managers some of the territory that Kouzes and Posner assign to leadership.

Kouzes and Posner talk a lot about values. Leaders, they claim, should embody values that followers admire. Many of their examples of major organizational change revolve around fundamental ways of working that require people to clarify or modify their core values. In the realm of values, there are few demonstrable facts and the changes advocated often entail a long, arduous journey. Such leadership amounts to a promissory note: if you have faith in my vision, you'll reap great rewards at the end of the rainbow. There is certainly a place for such leadership. It was vital in the 1980s when traumatic upheaval was needed to counter the Japanese threat. No doubt such leadership still has its place, but it can't serve as a general model of leadership in an age of continuous improvement and constant innovation. The four-box matrix below clarifies the differences between Kouzes and Posner's values domain and thought leadership.

Very little evidence	**C** Options with no clear right answer.	**D** Long term aims accepted on faith — changes in culture, values or complex technical projects with no evidence.
Hard evidence	**A** Immediate changes that are demonstrated to work.	**B** Ideas where hard evidence of viablity is offered.
	Immediate Implementation	Lengthy journey to implement

Box A Here employees advocate small changes to products or processes every day. Some such improvements entail changes in values such as in my example of a new help desk operator providing better help to users that colleagues could implement for themselves. Such leadership doesn't require a journey and doesn't ask leaders to clarify their personal values before showing leadership. In such cases, it's their technical or professional credibility that matters, not their personal credibility, integrity or values. In many such instances, good ideas speak so loudly for themselves that the leader doesn't need strong influencing skills.

Box B Here followers are invited to join the leader on a journey, as in Kouzes and Posner's model, but not one that demands a change in values. This is also thought leadership because what is being proposed is a complex new product or business model that will take a while to implement, substantial investment and the coordination of diverse specialists, as in building a supersonic passenger jet. But hard evidence is cited in support of such proposals. Because of the size of the investment, leaders in these situations must offer a solid business case using strong presentation skills. They may not need to make inspirational appeals to values to persuade followers.

Box C Some facts might be cited for one course of action over another but there's no hard evidence. Here, leaders need stronger influencing skills but they might still base their appeal on business benefits rather than values.

Box D Kouzes and Posner's model of leadership falls squarely into box D. Most of their examples of leadership entail lengthy journeys to change fundamental values for which there may be little hard evidence to support the proposed change. Here, the vision of leaders must be accepted on faith, so they must be personally trustworthy, transparent, committed and credible, as well as have inspirational influencing skills. The only basis for their influence is an emotional appeal to values because there's little evidence to call on. It's no surprise that this model of heroic leadership arose in the 1980s when drastic action was needed to radically transform U.S. competitiveness.

I'm not advocating that we abandon heroes, just that we turn more of our attention to new ones. These are the heroes that companies like 3M tell stories about, the champions of new products or business models that lead to major shifts in direction. It isn't this simple because I also advocate severing the connection between thought leadership and holding a position of power over people and that we strip away the managerial elements from our understanding of leadership that prevent it from being shown upward.

A close look at Kouzes and Posner's five leadership practices[5] reveals that only three of them fully pertain to leadership with only one being really core – challenging the process, the others being managerial practices:

1. Model the way
2. Inspire a shared vision
3. Challenge the process

4. Enable others to act
5. Encourage the heart

1. Model the way

Kouzes and Posner tell us that "modeling the way is essentially about earning the right and respect to lead through direct personal involvement and action. People first follow the person then the plan."[5] This principle is about doing what it takes to get elected to top positions in groups – executive roles, not necessarily one that implies real leadership. Modelling the way for Kouzes and Posner isn't a matter of leading by example on a specific issue such as personally delivering better customer service but rather of showing people what you stand for through personal dedication, transparency, how you treat people, hard work or commitment to a vision. Modeling the way ties in with one of Kouzes and Posner's views on credibility.

Because they see leadership as taking people on a journey, it makes sense to say that leaders must be personally credible. You need others to trust your promise to get them to the destination. But, if leadership is really about new content or substance, it's technical credibility that counts. As I explained using the matrix above, developing trust through modeling the way is only important in box D, hence it's a situational requirement not something to be generalized across leadership. I am not trying to minimize the importance of integrity, just to develop a general theory of leadership, one that applies across the board. The only generalizable feature of leadership is challenging the status quo, to promote a new direction. Sometimes you need to show integrity and emotional intelligence to influence certain people. Other times, this isn't necessary.

Personal credibility is more essential for management because being a manager means holding a position of power. We trust managers to deliver on our psychological contracts for job satisfaction, personal development and career progress.

2. Inspire a shared vision

This Kouzes and Posner principle has a leadership ring to it. With vision defined as a journey's destination, leaders can't expect to be followed if they don't know where they're going. But pushing to tweak a product may not be visionary. You could argue that all new ideas are visionary. But this is like saying that anything that has length is long or anything that has height is tall. Surely we reserve the word vision for ideas at the grander end of the scale. Having a better idea only counts as a vision if it's relatively long term and if it paints a picture of a rather magnificent future. New ideas can range along a very lengthy continuum from mundane, everyday good ideas to those that are revolutionary, radical and visionary.

Moreover, merely *having* a vision and using a *statement of vision* to influence people are two different things. A new customer service manager might have a vision of better customer service in her new employer's organization but might rely solely on leading by example, hence neither articulating a vision nor developing a shared one. This means that citing a vision was not the way the customer service expert influenced followers.

In addition, as we have seen, not all thought leadership entails a journey. You can change what people think to stop them from making a foolish error and you can convince people to change working practices that they can implement immediately, hardly a journey. Finally, leadership can arise spontaneously through brainstorming. It can be organic. Vision smacks of a mechanistic approach to setting direction where you can't act until you have a plan, a destination in mind. This makes no allowance for organizational learning conceived as figuring out what to do through experiment, trial and error. In this case, new directions *emerge* rather than being decided through prior, rational analysis. But leadership that emerges in the heat of the battle is still leadership despite not being visionary.

In short, hyping a vision is just one way of influencing people, useful for some contexts, not for others, hence vision can't be a necessary part of the meaning of leadership. Vision sounds like more of a leadership tool than one of management. Still, managers might motivate higher performance by periodically reminding employees of an existing vision. Using a statement of vision in this managerial, motivational way isn't the same thing as championing a new vision which would be leadership.

3. Challenge the process

At last we arrive at the core leadership principle. Kouzes and Posner state that all the cases of leadership they studied "involved a change from the status quo."[6] But they're very equivocal here, unfortunately so, because it's the main principle of their five that characterizes leadership. They start out saying that leaders are pioneers who "search for opportunities to innovate, grow, and improve."[7] They quickly water down this sound point by adding "But leaders aren't the only creators or originators of new products, services, or processes."[8] Notice the phrase "aren't the only". This implies that Kouzes and Posner really see leaders in formal terms, as the occupants of positions.

If you champion new directions outside a formal leadership position, you're in this "aren't the only" category of non-leaders. But, the phrase "aren't the only" is wrong because, *all leadership is informal* even when shown by those in formal positions and, of course, when shown by everyone else. Championing a new product is always leadership whether the leader is a manager or not.

Kouzes and Posner state that new ideas come from a variety of sources including "people on the front lines." But, for them "The leader's primary contribution is in the recognition of good ideas, the support of those ideas, and the willingness to challenge the system to get new products ... adopted."[9] This is a very watered down way of "challenging the process." Here the "leader" merely fosters the challenging of the status quo in employees. The reason for the equivocation is that there is no room in Kouzes and Posner's world for management. If they could embrace a constructive account of management, they could easily say that leaders really do challenge the status quo, leaving it to managers to do the supporting and facilitating of such initiatives from others.

So, "challenging the process" is the only one of Kouzes and Posner's five principles that is an essential feature of leadership and the only one that distinguishes leadership from management. But even here, I am saying something different from Kouzes and Posner, that leadership is precisely "challenging the process," never the support, recognition or fostering of such action in others.

4 & 5. Enable others to act, encourage the heart

I discuss Kouzes and Posner's fourth and fifth practices together because they're not hugely dissimilar. Both relate to enabling teams to reach the destination, empowering and motivating them to exert the effort. These two principles most clearly pertain to the implementation part of the journey and are the easiest to classify as management.

Starting to write in the 1980s, Kouzes and Posner are heirs to a constipated concept of management. Worse, their last two principles do not apply to bottom-up thought leadership at all. If you're showing thought leadership to your superiors and they accept your idea, then your leadership comes to an end as soon as they get on board. It isn't your place to "enable your superiors to act" or to "encourage their heart." Hence, these principles must be managerial – getting things done through people who report to you.

Conclusions on *The Leadership Challenge*

In summary, Kouzes and Posner wrote a great book about how to inspire people to undertake major change, a much needed recipe for the traumas of the 1980s. But they failed to question the ridiculous trashing of management, hence creating a bloated, confused view of leadership. They offer good advice on how those in charge of teams can engage and motivate people to undergo major transitions. But, as an explanation of leadership, it is dated.

Kouzes and Posner's view of leadership is one version of the wildly popular idea of transformational leadership. Bernard Bass developed a similar, more academic, version.

Transformational and thought leadership

Bernard Bass's leadership model has four components:[10]

- Idealized influence: be an admired role model.
- Inspirational motivation: be inspirational.
- Intellectual stimulation: stimulate creative thinking.
- Individualized consideration: support individuals.

Intellectual stimulation sounds a bit like thought leadership but the resemblance is superficial: "Transformational leaders stimulate their followers" efforts to be innovative and creative by questioning assumptions, reframing problems, and approaching old situations in new ways.'[11] But this theory is framed in terms of how the person in charge motivates followers to higher levels of performance. Stimulating others to think creatively is what managers do; this is nothing to do with leadership.

Strictly speaking, none of Bass's four components relate to leadership. Being an admired role model is partly relevant but it also overlaps with paternal and primitive leadership, our tendency to look up to people because of their magnetism rather than the content of their ideas. Individualized consideration is a management tool.

Influencing people to buy a new idea by paying attention to their needs is salesmanship not leadership. It's for the same reason that there is no such thing as transactional leadership. You can reward people for *doing* things but not for changing their underlying beliefs. To achieve the latter takes genuine thought leadership; people only change what they think when convinced.

Old wine in new bottles

The distinction between transformational and transactional leadership is really just old wine in new bottles as it's based on the older notions of showing consideration for people versus initiating structure.

> Being transformational is just "showing consideration for people" on steroids.

Both distinctions are founded on the premise that leadership is only displayed by people in charge. With this starting point, we move to the question of how such people move employees to be productive – is it about focusing on the task or the person? This whole line of thinking is outdated, a dead end for understanding leadership.

CHAPTER 8

Relationships: Women as Leaders

Leaders, followers and relationships

"YOU CAN'T BE a leader without followers" is an old truism. But what does it really tell us about leadership? What sort of relationship is there between leaders and followers?

A common leadership myth is that leadership is a relationship. This mistake arises because we focus on what goes on in working groups, overlooking leadership from the sidelines and front-line knowledge workers. I want to do four things here: show why leadership isn't a relationship, explore what is actually going on when people do work closely together, show how leadership is a one-way impact and, finally, discuss the implications of these ideas for the increasingly heard claim that women might make better leaders than men because of their relationship skills.

Why bother? Because making relationships central to leadership means that people with poor relationship skills and outsiders can't show leadership. The relationship model makes leadership a *closed* group activity, not something that can be shown across groups. If we genuinely want to foster leadership, we need to get rid of the clutter.

Leadership is seen as a relationship because it's a "relational" concept; it implies at least two parties. But as we saw in Chapter One, leadership can come from outside the organization where there is no relationship in the sense of team membership. We're still inspired today by long dead leaders. Some contemporary activists are inspired by Gandhi's non-violent style of confrontation. Millions of people are still moved by Martin Luther King to seek justice for minority groups or to promote equality.

Bill Gates is a follower of leadership shown by outsiders. He followed the lead of Apple in moving from Dos to Windows with its graphical user interface. He followed the lead of Netscape by introducing Internet Explorer, Apple again in offering a music service like iTunes and yet again with iPod. Finally, Microsoft is following Google in moving more heavily into search engine technology. Companies tell stories about their heroes, 3M with their post-it notes. Heroic tales inspire would-be heroes who never met their heroes let alone worked with them. This is leadership-at-a-distance with no working relationship between leaders and followers.

When you show leadership upward or sideways with people you don't manage, they don't depend on, or need to trust, you to look after them. Your bosses just have to buy your ideas. Having a relationship with people you want to lead can, however, help you influence them. It's well known that you need to build a relationship with the Japanese and Arabs before they'll trust you enough to buy your message. Hence relationships are a situational influencing factor rather than a basic ingredient of leadership.

The idea that leadership entails a working relationship with followers rests on a mistaken use of "relationship" anyway. Even thought leadership is "relational" in that it's an impact on a group and any impact entails at least two objects. "Impact" is a good example of a relational concept, unlike say, "table" or "car". "Eating" and "drinking" are also relational concepts. We can't eat or drink without eating or drinking *something*. So, "eating", "drinking" and "impact" are relational, but none of these implies a working relationship between people. Thought leadership is an impact and only a relationship in this logical sense.

The mistake here is to jump from the logic of relational concepts to the inference of actual working relationships between people, but this just doesn't follow from the mere fact that something is a relational concept. All the talk of the role of followers in our effort to understand leadership is based on this confusion.

The place of relationships

If leadership doesn't entail relationships between people, then what's going on in "grass roots" situations where people get things done with no authority to direct them? The answer: It's a *combination* of informal leadership *and* informal management.

Promoting new ideas about what to do is leadership. Organizing and implementing is management – even when the group is self-managing and everyone shares the managerial load. Management happens even if there's no one in a formal management role. It's the managerial function that requires close working relationships. Getting things done through people calls for close relationships to coordinate and motivate everyone involved.

But relationships also have a role to play in leadership.

> Relationships help at both ends of the leadership spectrum: to develop new ideas and to show leadership.

Leadership ideas can come from brainstorming within the team and from team members talking to competitors or customers, in all cases, good relationships help. Also, influencing some people is easier if you have a relationship with them, but this is a situational requirement. But these statements are a far cry from the traditional idea that leadership is necessarily a relationship with followers. Conversely, managers can't be effective at all without strong relationships with their team members.

Still, there's a feeling that complexity is driving us to base leadership on relationships. There's no doubting the need for closer coordination across diverse players to achieve complex tasks. Making a modern movie, for example, depends on a much bigger cast of characters now that so much technology is used for special effects. Innovation in the consumer electronics industry melds inputs from several parts of the business as well as customers.

Even artists, the stereotypical loners, study the work of their contemporaries, react to it or build on it. So, it's virtually impossible to work in isolation and hope to contribute anything of value to others. When you try to develop products on your own, you're using the now rightly disparaged "manufacturing mindset," thinking that you can develop something of value in isolation, hoping there must be someone to buy it.

But the argument from complexity only shows the increased need for aspiring leaders to work closely with others to develop new ideas. Relationships are key in the generation of leadership insights but not necessarily in the showing of leadership, bearing in mind that the source and target of leadership could well be different groups.

So, in what sense does leadership depend on working relationships between people? Leadership can be at a distance but is inspired by the ideas of others. Because the potential to generate good ideas is widely distributed, the ability of any one person to show leadership depends on the ability to network and brainstorm with diverse people. So, in the *formation* of new ideas, it helps if you can relate to people. The influencing of others to buy your ideas, the *showing* of leadership, also depends on relationship skills situationally. In some situations it helps to have good relationships to influence people, but other times, a strong case based on hard facts will do. Neither of these requirements for relationship skills forces us to define leadership as a relationship.

Why have some writers defined leadership as a relationship? A likely reason is simply that they have regarded leadership as being a type of person at the head of a group rather than as a function that can be filled by non-positional players. And they have lumped leadership and management together into one indistinct mass.

Why is this important? The simple answer: when fostering leadership in others, we need to emphasize having the courage to champion new ideas by whatever means, within reason. By making relationship skills definitional rather than situational, we risk discouraging introverted types from showing leadership – they get the message that they can't be leaders because they lack interpersonal skills. We need to be saying to them, instead, that such skills are icing on the cake, but if you can make a strong case for your ideas, you can indeed show leadership without such skills. This makes getting clear on the relationship issue vital.

Leadership as one-way impact

There is another argument that tries to show how leadership is a relationship. It takes the line that followers help to determine the impact a leader has on them, that it isn't just a one-way impact. So, it's argued, leadership must be a joint effort to determine new directions, not a one-way impact. Leadership, like beauty, is no doubt in the eyes of the beholder. So is influence. The most persuasive orator can enthral one person and turn another off even if both are good friends listening to the same pitch at the same time. But this is true of any one-way impact. If I drop a heavy book on my glasses, the impact is much different than if I drop the same book on the floor. So, the make-up of the recipient of an impact determines the effect of the blow. Clearly, some impacts can be two-way. Think of two similar size cars in a head-on collision where the impact is two-way, simultaneous and equal.

Leadership is a one-way impact. Proposals or suggestions are, by definition, made from one party to another. This is true even when we debate back and forth and influence each other by turns several times. In meetings, each participant takes turns showing leadership. It isn't about taking turns chairing, coordinating or facilitating the discussion, managerial ways to contribute.

Leadership is a particular kind of impact. As with any impact the make-up or predisposition of the affected object helps to determine the nature of the impact. But to say that leadership depends on followers doesn't entail that followers need to be *actively involved* in deciding how they'll be impacted. The same is true of taste in food or art. Two people who are otherwise alike might have very different tastes in food or art but it doesn't follow that the impact of foods or works of art is a voluntary choice.

The idea that leadership is relational is used to argue for shared leadership with equal participation between leaders and followers. But, if leadership can be at a distance, its impact is one-way, not something that followers necessarily participate actively in shaping.

There are important differences between the leadership impact and the example of dropping a book on my glasses. In the latter case, a book has the potential to have a consistent, predictable impact on any fragile substance by virtue of its having a set of fixed traits or properties, those relating to its mass. This isn't true of the leadership impact. Even the willingness to challenge others, the only constant trait across all instances of leadership, isn't fixed. Suppose you do not normally challenge others, but, in a meeting, you get an idea that is so obviously right, you can't avoid speaking up. Or, a person who is advocating an idea that you see as wrong might provoke you to speak up, thereby compelling you to overcome your normal disinclination to contradict colleagues.

Every other ingredient in your leadership moment is purely contextual – the subject matter, your knowledge of it, the stimulating ideas of others and how they behave towards you at that time. These ingredients are clearly not based on any enduring trait of your personality. This argument shows that your propensity to lead isn't, unlike my dropped book, due to a fixed trait within you, but something contextual.

Even your influencing style is situational. Your colleagues might be used to your being calm, warm and polite but now you're speaking forcefully and citing strong evidence for your ideas because something that someone said provoked you. The mere change from your normal way of addressing your colleagues could contribute as much to swaying them as the facts you cite. They might not have bought your ideas if they had been presented by a colleague who is normally assertive, but they're bowled over by the unexpected extent of your assertiveness in this instance. All of these points combine to show that, although leadership is a one-way impact, its success is very context-dependent and co-determined by the mind-sets and expectations of prospective followers.

But this doesn't mean that leadership is shared in any genuinely participative sense beyond the way in which the make-up of my glasses has a share in determining their reaction to a book dropped on them. Keep in mind that outsider leadership, because shown at a distance, is less contextual than the example here. Management, conversely, can be very participative simply because managers might fully share decision making with their teams.

Finally, it's worth noting that those who discuss shared leadership[2] are focusing on sharing the organizing, coordinating and motivating of colleagues for task achievement. This is shared management, not leadership, which definitely requires strong relationship skills.

A political motivation for exalting relationships

Some leadership writers base leadership on relationships for political reasons. They want to see more women in executive roles. If women have stronger relationship skills and leadership is really about relationships, then more women should be in leadership positions. But, all talk of positions is talk about management, not leadership. Indeed, relationships are far more central to management defined as facilitating the work of others. To get the best out of people, you have to help them achieve their full potential and this, surely, calls for acute relationship skills.

The relationship argument supports the drive for more women in *senior executive* positions, since such skills are vital for management, not leadership. There is no need to distort the concept of leadership to promote more women. See below for more on women as leaders.

Political leadership

Political leadership is relationship-based in another sense. To get elected, an aspiring leader must serve the needs of voters and cultivate a relationship with them. Voters delegate their authority to make decisions to the person they vote for, so the elected "leader" can make those decisions for them. Clearly, you can't get elected without appearing to meet the needs of voters (followers). Once in power, elected leaders can act as executives and make the decisions they like. But making decisions isn't showing leadership.

To say that there can be no such thing as a political leader without followers has a special meaning that doesn't apply to thought leadership. Thought leaders must influence people to accept their ideas but they do not need to *serve the needs of followers* in so doing. Their ideas might cause some followers to lose their jobs. In any case the ideas of thought leaders aim to serve the organization's needs to beat its competitors, not to serve the needs of followers.

In conclusion, why are these fine points important? Because they help to clarify for would-be leaders what they have to do to lead people. The current advice that relationships are essential, virtually by definition, is wrong. While you might work closely with followers, this is a situational fact, not part of the very meaning of leadership. Sometimes relationships will be critical to influence some followers, but other times leading by example, citing hard evidence, demonstrating a working prototype, expounding a vision or making a hard sell will be more effective.

Is leadership masculine or feminine?

There is a growing conviction that women are better leaders than men because we're moving from heroic individualism to relationships. Because women have these strengths more commonly than men, they should make better leaders, or so it's argued.

Would you agree that there is a continuum from being individualistic, dominance-seeking and aggressive, on the one hand, to nurturing, cooperative and supportive at the other end of the spectrum? The first pole is masculine, the second feminine, for men and women.

If we define leadership as challenging the status quo, those who show leadership could be anywhere along this continuum, but the majority are likely to be on the masculine side of the middle (men or women). People who show leadership are driven by a desire to differentiate themselves, but not necessarily to be the dominant person in a group. Some women are creative and iconoclastic outsiders. Being rebels, loners or outcasts isn't exclusively the domain of men. Feminine types have a range of influencing skills. Those without finesse rely on demonstrating a new idea or making a strong business case. But the urge to lead and the confidence to risk rejection by challenging the status quo is more of a traditional masculine trait, even if it isn't the exclusive province of men.

In *The Female Advantage*, Sally Helgesen doesn't draw a distinction between leadership and management. In her chapter "Women's Ways of Leading," she tries "to identify the specifics of how women manage."[1] Note the word "manage" used interchangeably with leadership. She addresses the questions: "How do successful women managers make decisions? How do they schedule their days? Gather and disperse information? Motivate employees? How do they delegate tasks?"[2] Helgeson uses the correct word when she refers to women as managers. For Helgeson, women are more caring than men. They spend more time with people, they network and see relationships as a "web of inclusion" not a hierarchy.

Part of the rationale for claiming that women might be better leaders than men is the shift towards a more interdependent world. But things are not so simple. Managers must have strong relationship skills to motivate employees, foster team work and sustain partnerships with stakeholders. But they also have to make tough, unpopular decisions. They need to challenge employees to stretch them. These tougher tasks require skills that are closer to the masculine end of the spectrum. The truth, surely, is that managers need both sets of skills rather than being either masculine or feminine. Managers need to get things done profitably. This means making hard choices as well as taking people with them. A balance of feminine and masculine skills would be better than being one-sided.

Actually, this whole debate between masculine and feminine virtues is just a new form of the old tug of war between "initiating structure" and "showing consideration for people", theory X versus theory Y, etc. where being masculine means to emphasize the task while being feminine means attending to the needs of people. The conclusion that a balance of the two is best is hard to dispute but not very helpful for being so general.

With respect to leadership, things are again mixed. Leadership has two fundamental aspects – one is the drive to challenge the status quo while the other is to win prospective followers. We could say that the former is masculine while the latter calls for feminine skills, but it isn't even this simple. Finding new directions to champion requires brainstorming and networking skills. Discovering leadership opportunities isn't easy for the lone wolf in today's complex, interdependent world.

So, now we have three leadership strands:

- Finding something new and useful to say.
- Having the courage to risk social rejection by saying it.
- Having a range of influencing skills to win support.

The first and the third strands call for relationship skills while the middle one requires a readiness to risk damaging relationships, especially when promoting radical ideas.

We tend to think in either/or terms – that leadership *either* means being dominant and individualistic *or* being caring, relational and supportive. There are two ways around this binary mode of thinking. We could say that people who show leadership have a balance of masculine and feminine traits, that it's *both* rather than either/or. Alternatively, it might be that the whole continuum is possible from one end of the spectrum to the other. Hence you can lead if you have poor relationship skills because you can satisfy the first two of the three strands. In this instance, you simply have to make a stronger factual case for your proposal if you lack other influencing skills.

Having feminine strengths and values might help you avoid upsetting people, but this should not stop you from showing leadership. You simply do so in a less aggressive, confrontational manner. If women do in fact have stronger influencing skills, should we therefore expect more leadership from women? Not necessarily, because influencing is only the means, form without content.

Self-differentiation is a masculine ideal. People with masculine traits are more driven to find something new and distinctive to say, even at the expense of relationships. But this doesn't mean that leadership is heroic and individualistic. Remember that thought leadership doesn't aim to dominate, just to promote new ideas. And no one can dominate in the world of rapidly changing ideas; hence such leadership is more egalitarian than hierarchical. Many thought leaders are not interested in status anyway.

In short, feminine traits are more essential for managers than for leaders. Recall the "level 5 leaders" of *Good to Great*: the core skills revolve around working with people, being modest, not being domineering or overly self-reliant and being able to facilitate a discussion to draw ideas out of others. Hence, "level 5 leaders" have some feminine traits. As I have argued, "level 5 leaders" are actually behaving as managers, not leaders.

A step deeper

Joyce K. Fletcher and Katrin Kaufer take the argument further by claiming that our concept of self needs to be recast, moving it away from its masculine, individualistic focus to one that is more relational, hence feminine. They criticize conventional views of adult development which "emphasize independence, autonomy and individuation, envisioning human development as a process of separation in which independence and self-sufficiency are the hallmarks of maturity."[3] In place of this conception of self, Fletcher and Kaufer argue that "growth ... occurs primarily through processes of connection. The hallmark of growth ... isn't increased ability to separate oneself from others but increased ability to connect oneself to others in ways that foster mutual development and learning."[4] Fletcher and Kaufer are not content to claim that increasing complexity and interdependence call for more feminine skills. They want to say that we have a distorted, one-sided conception of self.

Clearly, male models of self have dominated our thinking, but this doesn't require us to flip from one extreme to the other. On the contrary, it's a form of diversity to celebrate. You could argue that complexity requires a greater range of skills than any one person, culture or sex can offer. But this doesn't alter our conception of leadership. Diversity can foster better solutions through the blending of a wider range of perspectives. But leadership is a type of diversity itself – one person challenging an accepted idea. It's arguable that fostering diversity cultivates more leadership in an organization or community.

Ironically, this whole debate is old-fashioned by virtue of discussing what it means to be an *individual*, as if we really need a universally agreed single sense of self. This is like the one-size-fits-all mindset where corporations expect all senior executives to fit a single competency profile instead of celebrating diversity. One counter to this debate is to ask why we need one particular concept of self at all, regardless of whether it's an individualistic or relational sense of self.

My view that leadership can come from anywhere on the masculine-feminine continuum is consistent with my portrayal of leadership as contextual, that it arises in a context where it's stimulated to emerge by group and situational forces. Hence, it's less of a personal trait in any case. I would maintain, however, that there is a distinction to be made between leadership that advocates radical or unpopular ideas and that which is more incremental and readily acceptable.

It is not inconsistent to claim that leadership can come from anywhere along the masculine-feminine continuum while still maintaining that leadership at the radical end of the scale is more likely to emerge from people with more masculine drives. At the same time, in today's knowledge-driven world, working smarter is likely to be more successful than simply being aggressive. Women who find a way to challenge the status quo using excellent influencing skills could well show more leadership than men with their greater willingness to risk group rejection but with poor influencing skills.

A good case can be made, however, for promoting more women into senior executive roles. Clearly, relationship skills are important at all levels in organizations. There's also the argument from diversity to support this claim. But it should not be a question of whether men or women might make better leaders, executives or managers but simply that we need a better balance of men and women at the top if we want to reap the benefits that diversity can bring.

CHAPTER 9

Character and Emotional Intelligence

CHARACTER HAS EMERGED as a critical aspect of leadership, especially in the United States with its exposés of dubious leaders. It isn't that the U.S. has a surplus of less than morally perfect leaders. It's rather the low public tolerance for ethical indiscretion and a profit-hungry media that have brought the issue of character to the fore.

Character, integrity, values – all these admirable traits apply to the popular view of leaders as larger-than-life people in high places. But what does character have to do with leadership viewed as promoting new directions? Naturally, if we're wed to a paternal concept of leadership, we want anyone with power over us to have a trustworthy character and admirable values, but we must question whether this is genuine leadership.

The main point I want to expand on in this chapter, one I touched on a few times already, is that emotional intelligence and character are important for the rounded executive, or indeed anyone in a position of responsibility, especially when such positions include authority over people. Because leadership isn't a position or a responsibility, it doesn't require character or emotional intelligence, not at least in its definition. Where character and emotional intelligence come into leadership at all, it's only as influencing style.

The role of character and integrity in leadership

I argued that admirable character traits are not essential for leadership because it can come from cranky loners who we would not trust to run a meeting let alone a team or business. I also claimed that character and integrity are situational influencing tactics, not part of the definition of leadership. Character and integrity are essential to influence prospective followers when such conditions as these hold:

1. You need to be trusted to pursue desirable outcomes.
2. The personal cost to follow your lead is high.
3. Failure is possible and expensive – hence high risk.
4. Ambiguity is high; people depend on you to get there.
5. Followers can't get the benefits on their own.

When there's a lot at stake, you need to be trustworthy but also technically credible – people need to believe that you know what you're talking about. If you're leading by example, your trustworthiness and credibility speak for themselves. This applies to the bottom-up thought leader as well as the executive. For example, if you're in a software company, and you can produce a beta version of your software, character and integrity are not essential because you can demonstrate what you're advocating. On the other hand, if you're an employee at Boeing or Airbus and you're making a case for a viable supersonic passenger jet, you're asking people to join you on a lengthy, costly journey of uncertain outcome. Here, your success in influencing colleagues will rest on the following:

1. Your track record in delivering similar results.
2. Your knowledge of what is involved.
3. Your ability to make a convincing case.
4. Your visible conviction that this is the right thing to do.
5. Your integrity, character or trustworthiness.

The last condition says that people will need to trust you as a person in order to willingly follow your lead. The first four conditions imply that people need to trust your judgement rather than your character as a whole if they're to follow you.

Even in politics a Ralph Nader or other activist could influence us to change our minds and actions on sensitive topics thereby showing substantial leadership without our being willing to trust them to occupy an office of authority over us. This is another example of outsider leadership.

The character continuum

The importance of character in leadership lies along a continuum. The conditions listed above where character is important apply to situations where followers have a lot at stake. At one end of the spectrum are leaders who advocate changes that could have the greatest impact on our personal lives. Political leaders who base their mandate on the advocacy of key attributes of character, i.e. greater honesty, fairness, family stability, sensible use of money, selflessness, trustworthiness and accountability in public life need to be spotless themselves.

Conversely, sports or business leaders might have a slightly disreputable character in their personal lives, i.e. not always telling friends the truth or not always delivering on promises to their families but, so long as they play by the rules in their business or sport, they could still be seen as leaders. Some otherwise successful leaders are not as open or as accountable as we would like them to be. They occasionally blame others for their errors, for example. But so long as they maintain their professional credibility and can devise compelling new directions, people will follow them. We have followed some extremely disreputable characters after all – Hitler, Stalin and Saddam Hussein to name a few, not to mention criminal leaders. Keep in mind that leaders can be successful without being seen as good or admirable in the eyes of the broader world.

While we like to think we can judge character objectively, at least in the fullness of time, there is little doubt that character and integrity are in the eyes of the beholder. Followers of leaders many would judge to be disreputable could well be seen to have admirable character traits and integrity by their followers on the ground.

In any case, character and integrity are only necessary for leaders when prospective followers have a lot at stake personally. If there is no risk involved, say when the benefits are obvious, we do not care if we know those advocating the idea well enough to trust them. We can jump on the bandwagon of a great idea without knowing the actual leaders.

Consider eBay for example. The developers of eBay can be considered leaders in the field of online commerce but who knows or cares much about what they're like as people? You might object that their millions of admirers are customers not, strictly speaking, followers. That is true, but they're still a useful example of how we might similarly regard thought leaders who revolutionize our businesses. We're satisfied that their idea is a proven success. Some entrepreneurial leaders are slightly shady, but we follow them so long as they deliver and are professionally credible.

Character and management

Management, as an organizational role, is about having responsibility to deliver set targets and meet the expectations of stakeholders. Character, integrity and transparent values apply most especially to the managerial role. Employees depend on managers for some part of their welfare. Managers have power over employees, who expect to be treated fairly and openly. So, managers do need integrity or character to be effective in their roles. Note that, unlike showing leadership, this isn't a situational requirement. Management, by definition, entails responsibility for definable outcomes. This is also true of all non-managerial employees or indeed of any human role.

The amount of integrity a manager needs varies. Managers need to motivate employees to achieve higher levels of performance rather than to change direction. This means that, in some situations, employees will only be motivated if their managers have the requisite integrity or character. Specifically, the more cost or risk that managers ask employees to bear, the harder it is for them to motivate their teams. The classic case of managers who push their employees to work hard and then go golfing is a good illustration of the integrity gap that lets them down.

When little is at stake, the manager's confidence in employees can often carry sufficient motivational weight almost regardless of the manager's character.

Character and paternal leadership

Character is closely related to paternal leadership in Chapter Five because it's this type of "leadership" that engages our strongest feelings of dependency. Integrity increases in importance the more we depend on people to live up to our expectations. We overly invest the paternal leader with the power to make all things come out right and this upward transfer of power leaves us in a state of relative helplessness. In this frame of mind, we depend wholly on one person to save the situation. If we're let down, we could well feel that we have no alternative way of achieving whatever the leader had promised to deliver. When we put all our eggs in one basket like this, then the integrity of the (paternal) leader becomes paramount.

When we vent our rage on leaders we reveal as much about ourselves as we say about them. Our rage is as much a reaction to our own dependency as it is to the leader's alleged faults. We're more tolerant of faults in our friends if we have not created such a strong dependency relationship with them. As children we flew into a rage when our parents didn't let us get our way. And it's this same primal disappointment that compels us to lose our temper with political leaders if our relationship with them is paternalistic. We can no more accept that such leaders can be human than we accept it for our parents. Children see their parents as superhuman and we expect the same from leaders if we view them paternalistically.

Character has loomed large in recent discussions of leadership precisely because we're burdened with an overly paternalistic conception of leadership. We need to do two things here: Rid ourselves of this paternalistic dependency and reframe leadership along new lines. This isn't to belittle the importance of character for people in high office, but we need to depend less on such role occupants and to see them as executives instead of leaders. This isn't just a semantic shift. Calling such people leaders sets us up to depend on them because we're weighed down with an overly paternalistic conception of leadership.

Emotional intelligence and leadership

Emotional intelligence is now widely felt to be a central aspect of leadership. Daniel Goleman's book[1] on the subject has been a big seller. There are questionnaires designed to assess this capacity in people, along with courses to improve emotional intelligence. It's likely that the idea of emotional intelligence will have a long term, healthy impact on organizations if only because it's a clever re-packaging of vital truths that have long been known. Self-awareness and interpersonal sensitivity are obvious strengths for any manager, but calling them a type of intelligence adds to their appeal.

Goleman claims that emotional intelligence isn't only an important element in leadership; he actually states that his research "clearly shows that emotional intelligence is the *sine qua non* of leadership."[2] In other words, you can't be a leader without it. Unfortunately, Goleman doesn't define leadership, but it's evident from several of his statements that he doesn't differentiate between being a leader and being a senior executive or manager. This is especially clear in the following statement:

> Moreover, my analysis showed that emotional intelligence played an increasingly important role at the highest levels of the company, where differences in technical skills are of negligible importance. In other words, the higher the rank of a person considered to be a star performer, the more emotional intelligence capabilities showed up as the reason for his or her effectiveness.[3]

Senior executives tend to be older than junior executives and this fits in with the findings of Goleman's research: "One thing is certain: emotional intelligence increases with age. There is an old-fashioned word for the phenomenon: maturity."[4] This is, of course, a broad generalization to which we can think of exceptions. It's a similarly broad generalization to say that creativity and openness to change decrease with age. It follows from the general point about creativity that leadership should be more commonly found among younger employees – where leadership is conceived as finding or championing new directions.

No doubt some leadership on the part of senior executives does require the maturity of age in order to pick a new direction effectively and to influence others to get on board. Andy Grove's leadership at Intel has this ring about it. But a great deal of leadership occurs at the front-lines of organizations and is more entrepreneurial in nature.

Entrepreneurs are often not as "mature" as seasoned senior executives. But it's often the willingness of entrepreneurs to act somewhat irrationally, to take risks and to throw caution to the wind that enables them to demonstrate leadership. Entrepreneurs are notoriously insensitive to others, a bit eccentric. They can be up and down, angry and upset, impatient and overly driven, ignoring the needs of others at times. Their leadership consists in their applied creativity – the ability to devise new directions personally or by capitalizing on someone else's great idea.

> Contrary to Goleman, emotional intelligence (maturity) could not only fail to be an essential characteristic of leaders, it could actually get in the way of leadership in the entrepreneurial sense – simply because maturity is often a barrier to the sort of risk-taking that underpins the discovery of novel directions.

Maturity is associated with conserving energy, balance, seeing all sides in a debate, not rocking the boat and preserving harmony. These attributes are not commonly associated with creative risk-takers.

Indeed, surely emotional intelligence is a more important trait for managers and executives than it is for leadership. Managers need to achieve tasks that add maximum value with the greatest possible efficiency. This means getting the best out of people in relation to challenging targets. For this you need to resolve conflict as a referee. Here, emotional balance, empathy and self-awareness pay huge dividends.

Even executives who aren't entrepreneurial could be just as blunt and insensitive to others. There can be a high casualty rate among the colleagues of such executives who refuse to tolerate insensitivity. Still, they could excel in consistently being one step ahead of the market and thus regularly able to devise and sell winning new directions for the organization, hence showing genuine leadership. Again, emotional intelligence isn't part of what makes such executives effective leaders. Employees might not like such executives and they could follow their lead without a lot of enthusiasm, but if an executive succeeds in influencing the organization's direction, then leadership is shown.

Goleman might object that his research shows that the best performing executives do have emotional intelligence. The problem with this angle is that it fails to distinguish between executives and leaders. An organization can be a high performer in terms of market share and profitability in industries where competitive advantage isn't based on innovation, where success is due to excellent management. In such cases, little or no leadership might be required. In any case, we can agree that executives do need emotional intelligence. No doubt the Chief executives that Jim Collins studied had a high level of emotional intelligence, but most of their actions were managerial, not leadership.

Some leaders lead by example. They might not have the self-awareness to realize they're doing something that is exemplary and they might not care if others follow. So they lead without emotional intelligence. Conversely, many leaders are effective in the use of well-honed influencing skills. The stakeholders they need to influence could be particularly stubborn or resistant to the leader's proposal. The leader might have to bring together opposing factions in the organization in such a manner that all sides see themselves as having won something. In such cases, the leader needs emotional intelligence as an influencing skill.

Military leadership

How should we view the military commander who leads a charge against the enemy? This can be seen as a combination of leading by example and old-fashioned paternal or primitive leadership – deferring to the person who has the confidence of the group or the formal authority to order compliance. When the commander decides unilaterally to charge, we could call this a management decision, but actually setting an example, going first certainly counts as leadership. If the General, sitting in a remote command centre makes the decision, but stays away from the battlefield, there's no reason to call this leadership.

In more complex situations, such as choosing a business strategy, it's occasionally possible to lead by example, though not often. It's precisely this complexity that drove us to differentiate between sales and marketing. Leadership in complex, knowledge-based contexts usually requires equally complex arguments to move people and these can emerge bottom-up or from the sidelines. We get confused about leadership when we focus on simple situations like leading a military charge because we look at the person heading the group and what it takes to succeed in such a role. There's nothing wrong with analyzing personal traits to understand leadership but the question must be changed from what sort of a person can make it to the top to what sort of a person challenges the status quo.

In summary

Having emotional intelligence is a necessary condition of being a fully effective manager or executive. An insensitive manager can't hope to motivate people to give their best. Being an executive entails, by definition, holding a responsible role with power over others. This creates dependency. Being granted power over people raises the expectation to behave responsibly toward anyone reporting to you. For this, you need solid emotional intelligence, character and integrity.

CHAPTER 10

Leading, Influencing, Selling

WHENEVER YOU SHOW leadership, even unintentionally or by example, you influence someone to change direction. To be crystal clear about what counts as leadership and what doesn't, it helps to compare leading with other forms of influence like selling and teaching.

Leadership entails influence as shown by these circles:

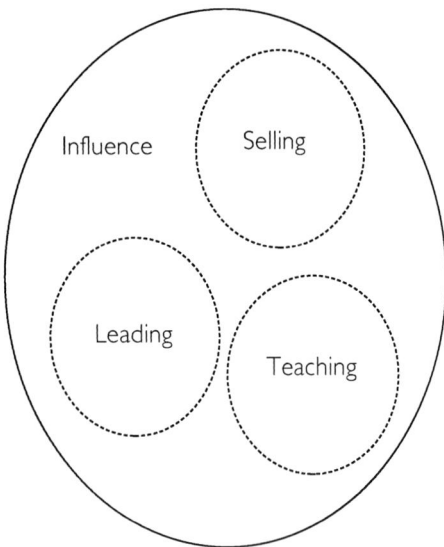

Everything in the large circle counts as influence – selling, leading, teaching and other forms of influence like coercion.

You can't lead, teach or sell without influencing people to do or believe something different. Each activity is in the circle of influence due to its impact on people and its purpose. If we just consider *impact*, we must say that teaching, leading and selling overlap.

This is because, when we lead people, we also sell them on the value of doing something different and if the idea is new to them we also teach them. But if we look only at the *purpose* of leading, which makes sense given our functional definition of leadership, then the three circles of leading, selling and teaching don't overlap.

This is because the purpose of teaching is to develop people and the purpose of selling is to put profit in the seller's pocket. Selling is done solely to benefit the seller. Leading aims to move a group to a better world, to improve its effectiveness. The purpose of leadership isn't to develop the group but to induce it to change direction.

So what? Well, leaders are often wrongly described as teachers. People no doubt learn from leaders as teaching is one type of influence or impact on them, but teaching is never the purpose of the leader. It's only a side effect. The sole aim of the leader is to induce a change in direction. When the leader intentionally instructs people, teaching becomes an influence tactic, not an attempt to develop them for its own sake or to improve their performance. Developing people to enhance their careers or skills is strictly a managerial undertaking. For leadership, teaching can be a means of influencing them, but never the aim.

When leaders have strong sales skills, they have a wider range of influencing tactics at their disposal. While some form of influence always occurs when anyone is led, using sales skills is only one style. For the same reason, parents do not show leadership to their children. Their purpose is to raise their children effectively, not to move a group to change direction. Persuading your son to eat his vegetables is certainly an act of influence, but not one of leadership.

The purpose of leadership is to move a group in a more productive direction. "Purpose" is interchangeable with "function". It doesn't matter then if the leader leads by example unintentionally. In this case, the leader's purpose is just to get the job done, not to influence anyone. But, if people copy the leader, say in serving customers in a better way, then leadership has been shown. We can still say that the leader's actions served the organizational purpose of generating a new direction even if the leader didn't personally intend anything of the sort.

What of coercion? Forcing people to do things counts as influence but never leadership. People in charge of groups might be bullies or tyrants, but in behaving this way they're not showing leadership no matter how effective they are in getting people to bend to their will.

A controversial case

What about persuasion based on an appeal to the audience's needs? What if a would-be leader sells an idea to you by showing you how it will make your work easier? Suppose this leader has tried to show you how the new process will benefit the organization but you were unmoved. You only get on board when you see how the new process delivers benefits for you. Is this leadership?

The solution to this puzzle lies in seeing the difference between genuine leadership and the actions of the person in charge. The latter may well persuade you to adopt a change by appealing to your needs, but this must be seen as a managerial tactic. To motivate people, the manager can switch between pointing to business benefits and showing you how the new process makes your work easier or more satisfying. But leadership influence must restrict itself to citing benefits for the organization. For example, aspiring political leaders who promise to reduce your taxes are buying votes not showing leadership. As soon as you flip from promoting organizational benefits to offering personal gains to people, you switch hats from leader to salesperson.

So, the counterintuitive claim here is that leadership influence can't appeal to the needs of the target audience, a reason to reject servant leadership, a topic discussed in Chapter Twelve. The value of this stance is that leadership always takes the moral high ground by relying on the promotion of change based solely on benefits to the group. Leadership influence, unlike selling, is never self-interested or manipulative. Hence subtle appeals to the interests of the target audience, which can amount to bribery, don't count as leadership despite the fact that doing so can be a highly effective influencing tactic.

This view ties in with the concept of thought leadership where it's only the logic of new content that counts as leadership. Regardless of whether a new idea is sold passionately or by a matter-of-fact business case, the focus is always on how the idea will benefit the organization. Otherwise, the influence attempt doesn't count as leadership even if it's effective. If your objective is simply to get a new idea accepted, why should you care whether it can be called leadership or not? Having your actions labelled leadership is like being congratulated. It's a prized label, not to be taken lightly or diluted. Restricting leadership to those influence attempts that rely on benefits to the organization preserves the intuition that leadership often works against the immediate needs of people. It asks them to make a personal or short-term sacrifice for the longer-term good of the group.

Clearly, however, there is no precise line between immediate selfish interests and long term group interests. When we sacrifice selfish needs, we postpone immediate gratification in hope of greater benefits later. But the same equivocation besets other concepts. Where is the border between tall and short, heavy and light? Without a precise border, we still understand the conceptual difference between tall and short, heavy and light. Similarly, we can make sense of the claim that leadership influence must cite long-term group benefits rather than the immediate selfish interests of individuals even though we can't establish a firm line between the two.

Leadership and creativity

Leadership and creativity overlap. Within the overlap, leaders are creative. They develop and promote their own ideas. When leaders are not creative, in the left circle, they champion the ideas of others rather than generate their own. Finally, the right circle represents, creative people, pure artists, who have no leadership impact. Their ideas are appreciated or valued for themselves without changing a group's direction.

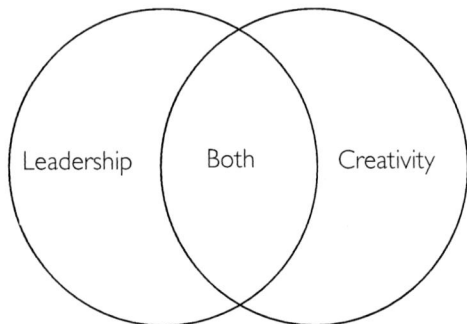

Creative people might not even lead their peers to alter their artistic style. It isn't that ideas are not enough on their own to lead people: leadership can be shown by example when followers are opportunistic and jump on the bandwagon with little persuading.

Process leaders are less likely to be creative than content leaders. Processes, like new ways of serving customers, outsourcing or other ways of cutting costs are easy to copy from one organization to another. Anyone who follows process improvements in other companies and champions them in their own organization shows leadership without being at all creative.

Content leaders champion new products, services or markets. They're more likely to be innovators although they can be early adapters of new technology too. This raises the question of how leadership overlaps with entrepreneurship.

Leadership and entrepreneurship

Entrepreneurs need not be leaders. They can be successful doing their own thing with little or no impact on others, starting a new restaurant, for example. Entrepreneurs can copy the ideas of others in starting a business. They share courage of convictions with leaders. They challenge the status quo but can be followers as well as leaders. They take risks to start a business or seize an opportunity but they do not necessarily champion anything especially new.

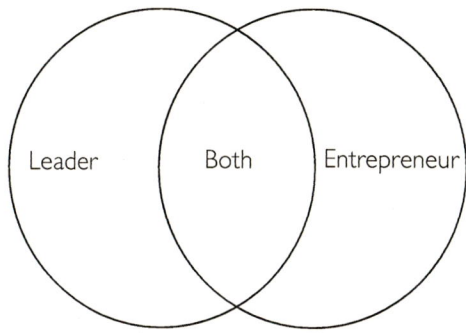

The founders of Google are examples of entrepreneurs who had a leadership impact on other internet companies like Yahoo! and Microsoft. The main leadership difference between entrepreneurs within and outside large companies is that the former have to make explicit bottom-up leadership attempts to get their ideas accepted. External entrepreneurs only lead large companies by example.

In conclusion, leadership is always a form of influence but never a particular style such as being inspiring or transformational. Leadership only gets identified with one influencing style when we focus on what it takes to get to the top of a hierarchy or when we see leadership in paternalistic terms. We regard charismatic people as heroes; we're seduced by powerful oratory. We need to set aside this temptation if we want to understand leadership, which must be defined independently of influencing style. This is the only way to make sense of the fact that leadership can be shown by example or with quieter influencing styles.

My point about the triumph of content or substance over form is relevant here. We need to restrict leadership to the promotion of something substantial – new whats or new hows that benefit the organization. Anything that amounts strictly to teaching or selling can't count as leadership.

CHAPTER 11

Organic or Mechanistic?

THOUGHT LEADERSHIP can be *emergent*, hence, like creativity, something that can't be deliberately managed, engineered or called forth at will. By contrast, developing skills in people – executives or otherwise can be engineered deliberately. Paralleling the difference between emergent and deliberate action is the distinction between organic and mechanistic conceptions of life in organizations. Leadership can only be fostered because it's based on youthful rebelliousness and because it's organic, which means that it emerges in the right conditions.

I have a number of ideas to develop in this chapter:

- Leadership can only be stimulated, not engineered.
- Leadership is partly organic, while management is mechanistic.
- Knowledge-driven businesses competing through innovation need to be more organic and less mechanistic, hence need to cultivate more emergent, thought leadership to prosper.

Leadership that is dispersed throughout the organization (bottom-up thought leadership) is organic because it emerges spontaneously and dynamically in widely diverse situations rather than being tied to a static role. There's a lot of talk about the need to achieve the level of flexibility of an organic organization but there's little appreciation for what this means for our popular concept of leadership. It isn't enough for the executive to be more flexible personally or to cultivate flexibility throughout an organization. We need to take a further step and rid ourselves of mechanistic notions of leadership. But first we need to see what it means to be organic and mechanistic.

Organic and mechanistic organizations

Just as organizations are advised to replace management with leadership, they're told they should get rid of their mechanistic cultures and structures for something more organic. The latter fosters greater innovation and flexibility, which mechanistic structures can stifle. However, we shouldn't abandon all aspects of mechanistic structures because effective management requires a high level of measurable consistency to obtain full value from an organization's resources. While we don't want rigidity, we still need efficiency and this requires a good degree of uniformity delivered through reliable processes.

In any case, being mechanistic doesn't entail rigidity except in extreme cases. The same point applies at a personal level. One person can be well enough organized while another is so organized as to be rigid. So, it's being excessively mechanistic that is the problem. In any case, being mechanistic means being planned, deliberate or controlled, not mechanical, thoughtless, ruthless, uncaring, robotic or routine. For example, coaching and empowering people are mechanistic in this sense simply because such interventions can be deliberately planned and executed, although what transpires in a specific coaching session is largely organic or emergent. That is, we can plan who we'll coach, when and how. We can set objectives and agree monitoring processes to evaluate the effectiveness of the coaching activity, all very rational and deliberate. This part is mechanistic. But the actual coaching conversations themselves are emergent by virtue of the unpredictability of what actually transpires in the meetings.

What does it mean to be organic?

The key feature of an organic organization is that new directions *emerge* from the front-lines rather than being decided on a top-down basis. An *emergent* direction is one that arises out of trial and error experimentation and feedback. By definition it is unplanned and unexpected. An organic solution to a problem is one that is *discovered* in action rather than decided through prior rational analysis. This form of organizational learning occurs at the edges of an organization where customer-facing staff interact with the outside world. Traditional, top-down planning is mechanistic because the organization is seen as a tool to be used at will by a thinking mind.

In an organic organization, definitive direction can't be known in advance of trying things out to see what works. Emergent directions are totally unexpected – such as when Honda switched their strategy for motorcycle sales in California from large to small bikes upon discovering public interest in the small bikes their executives were seen riding around town. In organic organizations, planning a new direction the way you choose your holiday destination goes out the window. Mechanistic and organic organizations are contrasted in the table overleaf.

Champions of the organic form talk of a win-lose battle between the forces of good and evil. But this is simplistic. Mechanistic organizations have competitive advantages in markets with a premium on low cost, efficient execution, where there is little competition on the basis of innovation. Organic trial and error action is wasteful and costly despite its advantages for cultivating innovation. Mechanistic organizations can be successful in their markets so long as there is sufficient empowerment to avoid the mind-numbing excesses of machine-like assembly line cultures.

While mechanistic organizations can make major changes, their competitive edge derives from improving how they deliver existing services or products rather than their ability to develop new ones. Process change, unlike innovation, can

Mechanistic organizations	Organic Organizations
1. Hierarchy of power	1. Power widely dispersed
2. Direction is planned	2. Direction emerges
3. Efficient, get things right	3. Learn through mistakes
4. The top thinks	4. Everyone thinks.
5. Control is engineered	5. Self-organizing
6. Defined roles	6. Loose structure
7. Clear boundaries	7. Vague boundaries
8. Compete on cost, quality, service	8. Compete through innovation
9. Value cohesion	9. Diversity is fostered
10. Uniformity, consistency	10. Variation prized
11. Central decision making	11. Extensive empowerment
12. Profits based on close cost control	12. Profits from new products
13. Change disrupts	13. Change is healthy
14. Experience is valued	14. New ideas prized
15. Leadership is position	15. Leadership emerges
16. Runs like a machine	16. Living organism
17. Rigid	17. Evolves
18. Static	18. Dynamic
19. Analyze, plan	19. Experiment, improvise
20. Rational solutions	20. Solutions discovered
21. Minimize risks, be safe	21. Take risks
22. Execute set plans	22. Entrepreneurial

be rationally planned rather than having to evolve through trial and error learning, except when you're developing a completely new process.

As you can see from the above table, mechanistic organizations are big on *control and rational analysis*, the conviction that every eventuality can be covered by sufficient analytical thinking in advance of acting, that good planning can prevent any untoward outcome. By contrast, an organic organization isn't deliberately controlled. You have to be comfortable to let the unexpected emerge with no prior notice, to seize opportunities that hit you with no warning, then to improvise as change springs unseen upon you. Conventional strategic planning is through and through mechanistic. The metaphor of the machine doesn't just suggest rigidity and efficiency. It also implies that no one in the organization does any significant thinking – it's all done by those at the top who operate the machine.

Mechanistic planning is like plotting the course for your organizational ship with a fixed destination in mind and then putting the ship on autopilot to get you there on time – totally futile if you're sailing on a sea where the shores are constantly and rapidly shifting and competitors are out to block your progress at every step. Or worse, where the very desirability of your original destination could change radically enroute. How can you plan your voyage fully before setting out in this context? It's only through recognizing the folly of such planning and capitalizing on the organic model that you can seize the opportunities that such a model of organizing affords.

A mechanistic organization is a tool that can be deliberately and purposefully used by someone who knows how to use it. An organic organization is a living thing. It has a life of its own and can't be manipulated or used as easily as a tool. It can only be cultivated or nourished, hence only guided to use its freedom for constructive ends.

The key to discovering the right balance for your organization between control and freedom is to be bold enough to conduct your own experiment. No one has the right answer for your organization at any given point in time. While you can look at any number of experiments in other organizations that seem successful thus far, you need to *discover* the best balance for yourself. However, you must buy a central aspect of organic organization even to start. Experiments, by definition, assume that what works must be *discovered*. To experiment in a fully open-minded way, however, you need to be comfortable with organic decision making at both personal and organizational levels.

Organic decision making on a personal level

We like to make decisions in a rational, linear fashion:

> think – decide – act

Such thinking is a linear process that ends in action. This is rational. Mechanistic organizations thrive on reason. Being in control means knowing what you want to do before acting. It avoids mistakes – the essence of efficiency, the god of the mechanistic organization.

Organic decisions are based on the feedback you get from acting, not from thinking prior to any action.

> act – get feedback – reflect – decide

Here, you experiment before making definite decisions. This increases variation (as in evolution), giving you unforeseen new options. It also enables you to see what works best before committing yourself. You can then reflect on your options before finally deciding. It isn't about acting randomly but rather being willing to take risks before you fully understand the implications of your actions and only making a final decision after you see what happens. Thinking in an organic way is uncomfortable for many of us. We hate looking foolish so we think through everything in advance of acting to minimize risks, to fully understand all the implications prior to lifting a finger.

For example, how comfortable are you going to an important meeting where there's a lot at stake without preparing yourself fully in advance? How comfortable are you approaching the meeting simply trusting your ability to generate a full, open dialogue, trusting that the best solution for all concerned will emerge in the meeting? This is group-level organic decision making. Better decisions will emerge in a group through brainstorming if participants do not come prepared with their own solutions set in concrete, with narrow, self-serving axes to grind, but are open to tackling issues on an exploratory basis.

As an example of personal mechanistic versus organic decision making, compare how you choose a holiday destination with making a significant career change. The former is mechanistic because you can make the decision without ever stepping out of your home or office. But when you think about your next career move and you want to do something quite different, you often feel stuck because it's like trying to decide whether you like a certain kind of food without tasting it. Career decision making is a bit like house hunting. You might start with some ideas about what you want in the way of a new house, but when you look at a few houses you see things you like that you hadn't thought of and you change your criteria.

So, deciding what house you'll buy is a process of *discovery*, unlike choosing a holiday destination. House hunting and career decision making are good examples of organic decision making where your final decision needs to be discovered through interaction with the real world rather than solely through prior, rational navel gazing.

Organization level organic decision making

It's hard to operate organically at an organizational level if you're loath to make your own decisions along such lines.

> To apply organic decision making at an organizational level, executives need to stop seeing themselves as the sole source of new directions. This is a key plank in my arguments that, in a complex, knowledge-driven world, at least soem leadership must be bottom-up and organic.

Instead, executives need to place more emphasis on facilitating exploratory thinking in others, creating the conditions for organizational learning to flourish. This is nothing new. We just need to stop the nonsense of calling such facilitation leadership. Organic decision making lies at the heart of effective organizational learning. Fostering organizational learning means acting in your market in ways that are not fully thought through, then revising your initiatives as you learn what works best. This entails introducing products quickly that are not fully developed and following them with upgrades as bugs are revealed and you learn what customers like about your products.

If you see organizational learning as relating, not to such messy trial and error learning, but rather to raising the knowledge base of employees, stuffing people's heads with information, you're operating with a mechanistic mindset. The knowledge management bandwagon is mechanistic unless it's based on organization-level risk-taking in the marketplace with a culture that celebrates action and learning from mistakes over cerebral storage.

Thought leadership is organic, emergent

To say that thought leadership is organic means that it emerges spontaneously in a specific context on an unplanned basis. This can happen in any meeting with colleagues, customers or other stakeholders. Ideas for new directions are discovered through brainstorming or trying out a hunch to find out what might work.

Thought leadership is organic on two levels. At the organizational level, it's organic because it isn't associated with formal position. It emerges anywhere within the organization or externally rather than emanating from a position. Hence, the source of an organization's leadership at any point in time is unpredictable. It could come from anywhere or several places at once.

On a personal level, thought leadership can be either

organic or mechanistic. Particular individuals might spontaneously show leadership in an unexpected manner in a meeting or lead by example without even being aware of it. This would be organic leadership at an individual level. On the other hand, someone with a great idea might undertake a deliberate, carefully planned assault on the status quo over a considerable period of time. A great deal of analysis might be put into formulating a strong business case, identifying what key players to target and how to influence them. This leadership is mechanistic by virtue of being deliberately planned.

More precisely, the decision to launch a leadership attempt might be spontaneous, hence organic, but the campaign to influence prospective followers is mechanistic. Thought leadership is fully organic when both the decision to show it and the showing of it are spontaneous and occur at the same time with no gap between deciding to show it and showing it.

This discussion shows why thought leadership can only be cultivated or fostered. Anything that is organic emerges spontaneously in the right context. It can't be deliberately decided or planned in advance. It isn't a matter of identifying thought leaders and slotting them into roles. First of all, there is the fact that thought leadership is more contextual than a fixed trait of individuals. Because no one has a monopoly on good ideas, thought leadership shifts with the wind from one person to another. It's totally fickle and ephemeral.

Secondly, a context such as brainstorming often deserves more credit for the emergence of thought leadership than the individual idea champion so it's hard to pin it down to particular individuals. Then there is the fundamentally organic nature of thought leadership and the overarching culture that it thrives in. The whole process of identifying people with specific traits for a structured role to meet a well defined need is mechanistic. It doesn't matter who shows leadership at any point in time, whether it's front line employees or the Chief executive. All leadership is organic or informal where, if there is a mechanistic element at all, it's only the influence strategy that is deliberate.

> The question organizations need to ask, therefore, isn't "Who has the potential to show leadership?" But rather, "How well does our organization foster and support the emergence of leadership?"

To say that management is inherently mechanistic isn't to disparage it. The decision to manage can also be organic or spontaneous among self-managing teams where one person sees that the team could be better organized and takes the initiative to get colleagues back on track. However, taking management action is always deliberate for the simple reason that, by definition, management is an organized rather than reactive type of action. Management is organized by virtue of always addressing the question of how to obtain a better return from all available resources relative to a specific task or objective. The essence of management, therefore, is deliberate, strategic action.

Management can be mechanistic in this sense without being mechanical, rigid or closely controlling. As we have seen, managers can be excellent coaches with an abundance of emotional intelligence and they can also be inspirational in their motivational style. Management needs to be mechanistic only in the sense of deliberately aiming to enhance the efficiency and effectiveness of operations in a planned and organized manner. Keep in mind that, though mechanistic in this sense, management isn't necessarily interferring or tightly controlling. Think of managing a delicate ecology where you can only tinker around the edges because any more intrusive intervention could be more damaging then constructive.

Practical implications

Like creativity, much of thought leadership depends on the inspiration of the moment and the right context. This means that the focus of leadership developers should be on the culture rather than putting individuals with suspected leadership potential through leadership development programs. You could object that the bulk of the leadership we're interested in is that which champions large scale change. This leadership, or at least the influencing strategy that accompanies it, is deliberate. People with the drive to lead can be deliberately developed by training them on sophisticated influencing tactics.

No question, influencing skills can be improved through training. And, of course, a good deal of large scale leadership initiatives will be mainly deliberate. My point is that, in an era of guerrilla warfare, this leadership can no longer be our paradigm case of all leadership. Organizations that depend on the creative thinking of all employees to survive need to cultivate spontaneous thought leadership much more proactively than they have in the past. This doesn't preclude old fashioned deliberate, top down leadership. It only argues that such leadership is no longer the main source of competitive advantage in the race to innovate faster than competitors. In this context, we have to be open to new directions wherever they emerge.

CHAPTER 12

Servant Leadership

SERVANT LEADERS allegedly lead by serving the needs of others; they put the needs of followers before their own. This theory isn't just saying that it would be nice if leaders *considered* the needs of employees. No, it's actually saying that serving is a core element of the very meaning of leadership. Not everyone has heard of servant leadership, but it's been around for 30 years or so. And its advocates claim to have witnessed an unparalleled explosion of interest[1] in the idea in recent years.

This concept is fundamentally confused however. It might apply well enough in the public sector, especially in professional associations and country clubs where serving the members is the primary reason for being. But it has no place in the private sector where the aim is to beat competitors. Here, serving the needs of organizational members gets in the way of meeting the organization's needs and this clashes with the leadership agenda.

Still, this theory offers itself up as a serious account of leadership and so it's worth a look.

The concept of servant leadership was introduced by Robert K. Greenleaf in 1970 upon reading a novel by Herman Hesse in which a group's servant emerged as their leader. It seems that the servant succeeded in keeping the group together and productive by tending to their needs and, when he left, the group was no longer effective. Defenders of servant leadership point to the values of the servant leader –

selflessness and service to others as attributes that many would like to see in leaders. They also point to the move away from command and control management to motivate modern employees. Liberated managers, they argue, motivate employees by serving their needs rather than focusing exclusively on their own agendas.

One problem with this view, however, is a failure to be precise enough about the meaning of leadership and how it differs from management. If leadership is related to service at all, it's about serving the organization's needs to beat competitors. Sometimes managers need to make employees redundant and hire more effective replacements to gain the needed competitive advantage – this is clearly not serving the needs of existing employees. Also, the leader often has to challenge the status quo to stir up dissatisfaction with current directions. Again, the leader must put the organization's needs first, not those of employees.

Leading employees is *only a means to an end* – the objective being to get them to do what is in the best interest of the organization. This statement directly contradicts the servant leadership proposition which "puts serving others – including employees, customers and community – as the number one priority."[2] But surely this is confused. The number one priority must always be to keep the organization viable. This entails putting customers first, which can result in sacrificing the needs of employees. Even if a manager unites organizational needs with those of employees, this is only a side effect rather than what it actually means to lead. The fundamental meaning of leadership is to provide direction, whether it meets the needs of employees or not.

Conversely, managers *do* need to look out for the needs of employees to motivate them to achieve challenging targets. Management means making the best use of all resources in the execution of set tasks. And employees will not be motivated unless their needs are met. But even here, the main priority is to achieve targets, so serving the needs of employees is again only a means to an end, not an end in itself. Managers sometimes have to challenge and stretch employees. Yes, you could say that this is indirectly serving their need to grow and develop. But in this case the notion of "servant" is at best misleading. Genuine servants who challenge their masters and put pressure on them to work harder would soon be looking for new masters.

Oddly, the advocates of servant leadership argue that they want to move managers away from a command and control mentality, but by using the terminology of "servant" they're still conjuring up master-slave imagery. Why not talk of partnership instead? Partners meet each other's needs in order to create win-win outcomes, but they cease being partners when one acts as the other's servant.

Some defenders of servant leadership argue that it isn't so much about serving the needs of employees that counts, it's more about having a generalized desire to be of service to some higher purpose than your own personal desires. This is of course a laudable attitude, but it tells us nothing about leadership per se. Doctors and other committed professionals also dedicate themselves to serving humanity, often at great personal cost to themselves. So, the desire to serve, by itself, tells us nothing about how a leader is to be differentiated from what it means to be any other hard-working professional.

To say that a leader is someone who wants to serve is like saying a whale is a mammal without telling us how whales differ from other mammals. Of course, many leaders have a desire to be of service to a higher cause, but unless we can be shown how this characteristic is a defining attribute of leaders uniquely, then we're no further ahead in our understanding of leadership. Thought leaders, as I have characterized them, are moved by a desire to do things differently, to be creative, to make a contribution. These are not narrowly selfish needs to gain a promotion or earn more money, but to call this servant leadership doesn't explain or add anything of value to our understanding of what it means to be a thought leader.

In other words, wanting to do something better or different could have as its basis curiosity and a desire to differentiate yourself rather than a desire to serve. A thought leader might not be driven by material rewards, but not being so self-interested doesn't translate into a desire to serve a higher cause. Usually, thought leaders have an intrinsic interest in their subject which can hook them to the extent that they neglect food, sleep, bathing and other self-interested motives. To call this a desire to serve is to water down the concept of service beyond usefulness. In any case, the move to a generalized desire to serve a higher cause is a distortion of the original idea of servant leadership which was about serving the needs of followers.

However, as I argued in Chapter Ten, to appeal directly to the needs of prospective followers isn't leadership at all – this is merely buying votes. Buying the support of followers by attending directly to their needs is being a salesperson not showing leadership. This ties in with my point about saying a whale is a mammal without telling us how it differs from other mammals.

My specific challenge here is this: How does being a servant leader differ from being a sales person? Suppose you're selling timeshares in sun-drenched holiday homes. You appeal to your prospect's higher lifestyle needs but your ambition is selfish, to line your pockets. While many political leaders genuinely want to improve the world, they must also appeal directly to the needs of their prospective voters if they're to meet their own desire to get elected. This makes such leadership closer to salesmanship than thought leadership which can point exclusively to the benefits of a product for customers regardless of its impact on employees or executives (followers). Some of the latter could in fact lose their jobs if the proposed new product cannibalizes existing product lines.

The idea of serving others could well apply to political leaders or civil servants as it's their role to serve the needs of the public. Political leaders don't run competitive enterprises, so they can focus exclusively on the needs of those who elect them – their followers. In fact, as I noted earlier, political leaders can't get elected without being seen to serve the needs of a range of followers. So, being servant-like is essential for the would-be political leader.

Further, many public service organizations have, as their defining purpose, to serve the needs of their constituents. This is always true in charitable organizations, clubs and associations. To be a leader or executive in such organizations may well require a mission to be of service. But this is a requirement for one particular leadership situation, not a universal truth of leadership across all contexts. And it's the latter that I'm trying to develop.

In conclusion, the idea of servant leadership has nothing useful to tell us about how to lead a competitive business. Managers might be better at motivating performance if they were more inclined to serve the needs of their teams, but even here the term "servant" is at best an exaggeration. Managers and employees are often portrayed as partners today and, certainly, the concept of partnership is a very sensible one. The use of the term "servant" is going from one extreme to the other – from the manager as dictator to that of servant. While modern managers might no longer be tyrannical dictators, they're not usefully regarded as servants either. Partner, yes, servant, no.

CHAPTER 13

Leadership with a Postmodern Twist

THE TITLE of this chapter is meant to convey the message that organizations today have some postmodern elements or twists without compelling us to embrace all aspects of postmodernism. The bottom line is that we need a mix of modernist rationality and postmodern non-rationality (as opposed to irrationality). Put simply, we need both the analytical, rational efficiency of management along with the less rational, spontaneous, emergent creativity of leadership to be successful. This is the same point I was making in Chapter Eleven when I argued for a balance between mechanistic and organic organizational forms.

The rationale for this chapter is to pull together the various bits of things I have been saying about leadership into a coherent whole, to present as clear an image as possible of how we ought to think about leadership and management in the future. An important subsidiary theme I want to discuss is anxiety – caused by feeling out of control and losing our sense of where we're going. The modernist world that postmodernists reject is one of relative certainty and rationality where we felt we were in relatively firm control of our destiny. Today we have to cope with the pressure of rapid change and complexity, a situation made worse by the vague dread that there might be no solid anchor or base to grab hold of to get our bearings and reduce our anxiety.

The ultimate aim of this discussion is to make it clear how we can address this anxiety while still embracing important changes in the way we think about life in organizations. My objective here is to argue that we need to rely more on ourselves and each other, placing less reliance on leaders-as-saviours to look after us.

Briefly, the postmodern critique can be summed up as an attack on all forms of authority. This way of looking at postmodernism gives us a link to what I have said about the need to switch our understanding of leadership from positional power to something diffuse, spontaneous, unpredictable, ephemeral and free-floating. What I want to guard against is the rejection of this new way of viewing leadership because it's anxiety-producing when what we should be doing is finding better ways to deal with our anxieties relating to loss of control, rapid change and chaos.

Outline of postmodernism

Chief claims of postmodernists include the following:

- Nothing is certain. Everything is perspective, including science.
- There is no objective knowledge, only competing interpretations.
- There is no progress, just a proliferation of different viewpoints.
- There is no authority over what is right and wrong.
- We must accept diversity as no single view is true.
- Human reason is limited; a lot depends on non-rational factors.
- There is no autonomy, all is community.
- The physical universe isn't an ordered machine.
- There are limits to how much we can predict or control. We must simply let some things evolve and try to nudge them along in our preferred direction.
- There is no ultimate authority on fundamentals.
- The group and the identity it once provided us is now fragmented, disjointed.

Postmodernism isn't quite the rage it was a few years ago, but many of its core themes have made deep inroads into our thinking about organizations. If you find the idea of postmodernism a bit extreme, keep in mind that, if all is interpretation, then so is postmodernism and we're hence free to regard it as we see fit. Whatever the future of postmodernism as an all embracing story, we're no longer as confident in our modernist assumptions as we once were.

Modernist and postmodernist themes

In the table below, I set out a few of the more telling contrasting themes to show some of the ways we're leaving modernism behind.

Modernist themes	Postmodernist themes
1. The boss knows best	1. No one knows best
2. Strategy is a linear plan	2. Strategy can emerge
3. Central control is best	3. Empowerment is best
4. Team work vital	4. Diversity vital
5. Leaders decide	5. Decisions emerge
6. Get it right first time	6. Take risks and learn
7. Plan all action fully	7. Improvise
8. Organizations are machines	8. Organizations are organisms
9. All can be managed	9. Some things evolve
10. We control our destiny	10. Our destiny emerges
11. I identify with my organization	11. My identity is fragmented
12. Decisions precede action	12. Decisions emerge
13. Stability is good	13. Success breeds failure
14. Clear boundaries	14. Boundarylessness
15. Communication flows through hierarchy	15. Communication flows through networks
16. Success comes through applying knowledge we have in our heads	16. Success comes through seizing the right opportunities

Modernist themes	Postmodernist themes
17. Emotions have no place in a rational organization 18. Managers appeal to reasoned self-interest to motivate performance 19. We rely on our superiors to look after our careers 20. Employee retention is desirable 21. Leadership is a role or position	17. People act on the basis of emotional drivers 18. Managers arouse people's basic emotional drivers to inspire them 19. We need to manage our own careers 20. Retention hinders innovation 21. Leadership is an occasional act

Clearly, these lists could be extended almost indefinitely. But we have enough to throw into sharp relief the reasons for anxiety for both executive and employee. Executives feel they're losing control and employees aren't sure they want the responsibilities that once clearly rested only on executive shoulders. For the latter, it's a repeat of how they felt when they first left home – a combination of liberation and fear of failure without the security blanket of parents to smooth over the scrapes. We actually want it both ways: the freedom to determine our own destiny but someone in charge to fall back on when things get difficult or when we're unsure of ourselves.

A way ahead

We think in binary, either/or terms: if one way of looking at the world is wrong, we must reject it for something totally different. The reality is, however, that we need to find the right combination of the old and new to be successful and this balance will be different for every organization. Recall that organizations have two different tasks:

- To make a profit or achieve expected results today
- To create the future

The first objective requires us to act in a modernist (mechanistic) manner while the second task forces us to embrace some elements of postmodernism (being organic).

We need to combine efficiency and creativity in one body. But this only seems odd if we're wedded to seeing organizations as unities, as single individual entities rather than as loosely coupled confederations or partnerships with porous, shifting boundaries. Instead of authority flowing down the hierarchy, it's now vested in diverse interest groups that pull together only as needed. Hence it's no longer the vision of one person at the top that drives everyone but a diversity of local imperatives that do not always complement each other.

Postmodern management

Efficiency depends on machine-like consistency, important for cost control but also to ensure uniform levels of quality and customer service. Effective management is essential for this task but it can be updated in line with a postmodern way of working. This means accepting that management as a function doesn't imply excessive top-down control by one or a few persons over everyone else. Yes, some success parameters must be centrally stored and analyzed, but the management function can be widely dispersed through extensive empowerment and self-management.

This is what Jim Collins means in *Good to Great* when he talks about fostering discipline to replace top-down, control. So, management becomes less controlling for this reason but also because it's more facilitative than directive. The effective manager is a coach, not someone who makes all the decisions and operates a machine. Further, management as a dispersed activity, shared by everyone, also has an organic dimension because all team members can spontaneously take charge to coordinate the efforts of their colleagues.

Hence management isn't as controlling as Abraham Zaleznik claimed.

Postmodern leadership

Much of what I've said about leadership has a postmodern dimension. Thought leadership is dispersed throughout the organization and can be directed up as well as sideways and down. It has nothing to do with role or position. Being a function, it's up for grabs by anyone who feels the urge and has the nerve. It's spontaneous, like creativity. No particular style of influence has anything to do with the meaning of leadership. You don't have to be inspiring or transformational even though it helps in some situations. It isn't necessarily as rational as setting out a destination for a journey. Thought leadership emerges in a context such as brainstorming where the context itself deserves as much credit as the individual's personal traits.

Leadership to promote radical change is a function of youthful rebelliousness rather than a growing maturity and set of skills you acquire incrementally throughout your career. My view of leadership is consistent with the idea that some organizational direction must emerge through front-line trial and error rather than being decided on a top down basis. It's primarily organic, like guerrilla warfare, rather than rational, deliberate, mechanistic or modernist.

Balancing the twin organizational tasks

There is no formula. Organizations that compete mainly on cost, service and quality and which are functioning quite efficiently at the moment need to be well managed and don't need much leadership. Conversely, those that either compete on the basis of rapid innovation or need to undergo substantial change to improve efficiency need more leadership. The point here is that it isn't about individual executives being equally good at both management and leadership. While some may be, others are likely to have stronger skills on one side of the fence than the other. But if leadership and management are dispersed throughout the organization, it doesn't matter in any case. To ask how an organization can be so different at the same time is to assume that an organization is, or should have, a level of internal consistency that is unrealistic. To think otherwise is to be locked into the past when the solid group was the lens through which we viewed leadership.

While a single person might not be equally effective at leading and managing, organizations have strengths across often great numbers of people. Embracing the postmodern organization makes it easier to see how a single company can be both efficient and creative at the same time. It isn't a matter of expecting individuals to have opposing traits but of having parallel processes that anyone can organically align with as required and in accordance with their talents.

The postmodern organization has no place for paternal or primitive leadership because it demands that we move away from reliance on authority. Leaning on a strong parental figure to cope with anxiety has the same advantages and disadvantages as drugs or other crutches. We might not find it easy to rid ourselves of the need, but we must strive to throw away our crutches if we want our organizations to prosper in the face of rampant competition. Whenever we let someone dominate us, whether informally, as a team leader or as a chief executive, we're abdicating authority and responsibility to them. But efficiency demands specialization so we can't avoid some upward delegation. Thought leadership, however, can't be delegated as it isn't a role. It's everyone's function. Once we set aside primitive and paternalistic models of leadership, we have only the generation of new directions and their execution to consider to understand leadership and management.

The fading fortune of the group

Our model of leadership is distorted by our focus on groups because it leads us to study the person who emerges as the most influential within the group. Postmodernism suggests that group boundaries are breaking down and that we should pay as much attention to intergroup dynamics as we do to what happens within them.

Consider the following three themes:

1. How group goals have shifted from (a) stability through (b) efficient production to (c) the ability to change fast.
2. How the forces that move groups have moved away from the personal power of the group leader to all manner of forces external to that individual's control.
3. How the boundaries between groups are breaking down.

1. The shifting of group goals

The objective of a primitive tribe or group of higher primates is subsistence – to eat and reproduce free from external threats. Leadership in such groups is clearly a position and relatively stable. Being a leader means having the power to attain and hold the top slot. Such groups do not have a product; they do not make or even do anything other than what it takes to survive. Stability, not effective change, is the measure of success.

By contrast, the goal of early business groups was to produce a product efficiently. It wasn't enough simply to exist as a group and do nothing. Successful forward movement is also required for the person in charge to be seen as an effective leader. Now leaders needed to accomplish two things: they had to display enough power to gain the top position in the first place. Then they had to get the group producing its product effectively. In this context leadership researchers had two questions to answer:

- What does it take to make it to the top?
- How to you get a group producing effectively?

Since the early 1970s, businesses have had a third goal beyond efficient production of a product and that is to continually evolve to keep up with a rapidly changing environment of aggressive competitors and rapidly shifting customer demands. Now, efficient productivity is the new stability and effective leadership must be aligned with engendering successful change. Unfortunately for positional leaders, this shift in group goals destabilizes their power base for the simple reason that the world is now too complex for any one person to figure out what to do next. Brute strength was once enough to hold onto a leadership position, followed later by the force of larger than life personality, but now there is the added pressure to divine new directions fast while wearing a blindfold. A wide range of other voices are now crying out to be heard.

2. The shifting forces that move groups

In primitive groups it was not safe to challenge authority. Death or excommunication surely followed. As recently as the time of Galileo and Martin Luther, questioning received wisdom was done at great personal risk – you could be burnt at the stake. Leadership in this world was a win-lose monopoly. Either you had the power to topple the leader or you paid the ultimate price. You could take the safe option and say nothing of course. Even in our time, Nelson Mandela was imprisoned for his challenge to the status quo while Martin Luther King was assassinated.

In politics, deeply held values cause seemingly irresolvable conflict, making change nearly impossible. Not so in business where rapid change driven by innovation is unstoppable. The point here is that, for groups that operate in an innovation-driven world, new ideas are the motor that propels change and, most critically, such ideas can come from any source other than (but not excluding) the person in charge of the group. This rise to prominence of external group forces complements the group's new goal of continually reinventing itself discussed above where no single person has a monopoly on good ideas.

3. Breakdown of group boundaries

In primitive times, when two groups clashed, one was defeated and the leader replaced by the winner. Much the same still happens today when a company is acquired. But in modern business, it's possible for several groups to compete in the same markets without any of them getting acquired or killed off. Winning has become less absolute, more relative. This makes business like a multi-team sports league where one team is temporarily in the lead and others sit for a while in second or a lower place. In this context, lower ranked groups look to their betters for leadership which means that their main source of leadership need no longer be the person in charge of their own group. Rapid change and growing complexity have also led to strategic alliances and complex outsourcing arrangements where it's unclear who is leading whom. Further, employees are unsure who is their leader in such complex marriages. Who is an outsourced employee's formal leader? With what group do such employees identify or belong?

Implications for leadership

The implication of the shifting fortunes of groups is that we can no longer restrict our efforts to understand leadership to the dynamics *within* groups. We now need a concept of leadership based on a much wider set of dynamics. The traditional small group, such as the street corner gang is *closed* in the sense that direction and power revolve around the one person acknowledged as the group's leader. By contrast, innovation-driven organizations in multi-firm markets are much more *open* to outside influences.

> Studying what happens *between* groups yields a vision of leadership divorced from position.

What does it mean to be a CEO in this revised leadership framework? There's no need to display leadership if new directions are not required. Industries that, relatively speaking, major on service, cost and quality, rather than rampant innovation, need effective management and not so much leadership. Even these organizations, however, still need leadership to champion continuous process improvement ideas. On the other hand, all CEOs admired by their organization members display primitive or paternal leadership. There is nothing wrong with acknowledging a legitimate place for someone to help employees allay anxiety, but it's confusing and dated to call this leadership.

Dealing with anxiety

The short answer to the problem of anxiety is to leave behind the modernist's excessive individualism. You might see yourself as a team player and you might identify strongly with your organization, but still place too much emphasis on your individual contributions. You like to think through issues yourself, make decisions and present solutions to your colleagues. Your confidence is based on your ability to analyze the content of your work and to offer well judged solutions. This pattern is as common for senior managers as it is for junior, technical employees. The result is that individuals take upon themselves more psychological ownership than is healthy.

While we don't want to abandon individual accountability to get things done, it's constructive to share ownership for decision making with others by placing at least an equal emphasis on drawing solutions out of them. An excellent way to engage others in your thinking and solution generation is to ask them questions about what they think, what they might see as options and the pros and cons of those options. Although thought leadership is the presentation of novel solutions, they don't have to be generated on an exclusively individual basis.

Too many managers think they're involving employees in their work by being good delegators of *tasks*, but they reserve all the key thinking and decision making for themselves. They sell their own solutions rather than create the level of dialogue that would lead to joint solutions. By thus being too individualistic, they set themselves up to be overly self-reliant and hence to have to face the anxiety of uncertainty alone. They see the role of manager as one of being decisive, on top of everything and as having most of the answers. Such executives love having people ask them what to do and to provide definite answers in return. Being able to contribute this type of input makes them feel useful, valued and confident. But, at the same time, they disempower others by fostering dependency. By behaving like this, they fuel their own anxiety because they know in their hearts that a great deal is too uncertain for them to have all the answers.

Evidence that anxiety is caused by excessive individualism emerges when managers attend development programs and discover that others worry about the same or similar things they worry about. This comes as a great surprise and relief because they're so used to operating individualistically on the job that they think something is wrong with them for feeling anxious. Others appear to be getting on with things comfortably while only they're worrying. It isn't totally their fault, of course, as organizational cultures excessively reward individual achievement.

Dealing with the anxiety of rapid change and a loss of control is partly about creating more fully shared ownership. But it can also be lessened by a clearer set of expectations around management and leadership, what they mean and how to engage effectively in them. Not having to shoulder all the leadership burden can help, but also shifting the emphasis of management from being the ultimate decision maker to a more facilitative, coaching style of working can help enormously as well. That is, the questions that managers can ask to facilitate decision making can be asked no matter what the content under discussion. It's much easier to base your confidence on such transferable skills than on your specific knowledge and ability to come up with the right solutions across diverse, complex situations.

Conclusions on the 7 leadership myths

Here are the seven leadership myths again:

1. Leadership entails taking charge of people.
2. Leaders are transformational, managers transactional.
3. Leadership is a set of skills that anybody can develop.
4. Leaders require emotional intelligence and integrity.
5. Managers should be replaced by leaders.
6. Leadership entails working relationships with followers.
7. Great leaders soothe our anxieties.

Torching the first myth burns all the rest as well, because leadership freed from position becomes a free-floating initiative that is independent of influencing style. This makes being transformational or displaying emotional intelligence a matter of situational influencing style, not essential for showing leadership. By defining leadership as an act that promotes new directions and nothing else, something that can be done with a variety of styles, it becomes clear that courage of convictions is the essential trait required to show leadership. Everything else is the means or vehicle to get people on board. Leadership divorced from position allows us to better understand leadership-at-a-distance and to clarify the status of relationships.

But the whole effort to develop a new understanding of leadership along these lines depends on a revitalized concept of management that can carry much of the load previously allocated to leadership. Managers can't be replaced by leaders as stated in the fifth myth.

Critically, we must be rid of paternal or primitive leadership even if we persist in looking up to people in high places and relying on them to soothe our anxieties.

The argument has been long and complex. Revamping such a convoluted concept can't be fully achieved in one go. Fostering a culture with a postmodern dimension, one that cultivates a more constructive concept of management and a dispersed form of leadership is both a challenge and an opportunity. As a challenge, there's the added anxiety for executives that arises through losing control and status. But the opportunity is liberating, both for executives and other employees. Executives gain a clearer focus on how they can best add value instead of feeling that they have to be all things to all people.

All employees can show leadership now, rather than having to wait to be promoted and even if they never want to be managers. The organization benefits through better use of all its talent, more sharply focused executives and more employees thinking of possible new directions to keep the organization relevant in the future.

Notes and References

Introduction
1. James M. Kouzes and Barry Z. Posner, *The Leadership Challenge*, Jossey Bass, Third Edition, 2002.

Chapter 1
1. Gary Hamel, *Leading the Revolution*, Harvard Business School Press, 2000, page 25.
2. These examples and names are fictitious. So are those in other examples, John Wells and Tom Bower. In the latter two cases, I use the techniques of fiction writing to make the book as reader-friendly as possible.
3. Seth Godin, *Permission Marketing*, Simon & Schuster UK Ltd., 2002.
4. Kouzes and Posner, page 156.

Chapter 2
1. Abraham Zaleznik, *Managers and Leaders: Are they different?* Harvard Business Review on Leadership, Harvard Business School Press, 1998.
2. Abraham Zaleznik, *The Managerial Mystique*, Harper & Row, 1989, page 62.
3. Zaleznik, 1989, page 65.
4. Zaleznik, 1989, page 75.
5. Zaleznik, 1989, page 67.
6. Zaleznik, 1989, page 74.
7. Zaleznik, 1989, page 71.
8. Zaleznik, 1989, page 72.
9. Zaleznik, 1989, page 28.

10. Warren Bennis and Bert Nanus, *Leaders, Strategies for Taking Charge*, Harper & Row, 1985.
11. Joan Magretta, *What Management Is*, Profile Books Ltd, 2003.
12. Magretta, 2003, page 15.
13. Magretta, 2003, page 5.
14. John Kotter, *A Force for Change, How Leadership Differs from Management*, The Free Press, 1990.
15. Kotter, 1990, page 7.
16. Sandy Weill, quoted in Thomas J. Neff & James M. Citrin, Lessons From The Top, Penguin Books, 1999, page 335.
17. Thomas J. Neff & James M. Citrin, 199, page 188.
18. Jim Collins, *Good to Great*, Random House, 2001.

Chapter 3
1. Gary Hamel, 2000, page 13.
2. Gary Yukl, *Leadership in Organizations*, Prentice Hall, Fourth Edition, 1998, page 6.

Chapter 4
1. Ronald Heifetz, *Leadership Without Easy Answers*, Harvard University Press, 1999.
2. Noel Tichy & Stratford Sherman, *Control Your Destiny or Someone Else Will*, Harper Business, 1994, page 254.
3. Tichy & Sherman, 1994, page 277.
4. Tichy & Sherman, 1994, page 278.
5. Tichy & Sherman, 1994, page 247.

Chapter 5
1. Roger Lewin and Girute Regine, "An Organic Approach to Management", Cap Gemini Center for Business Innovation Journal, Issue 4.
2. Arnold M. Ludwig, *King of the Mountain*, The University Press of Kentucky, 2002, page 1.
3. Ludwig, 2002, page 8.
4. Nigel Nicholson, *Managing the Human Animal*, Thompson, Texere, 2000, page 98.
5. Nicholson, 2000, page 98.
6. Nicholson, 2000, page 100.
7. Nicholson, 2000, page 109.
8. Abraham Zaleznik, *The Managerial Mystique*, Harper & Row, 1989, page 150.
9. Zaleznik, 1989, page 151.

Chapter 6
1. Kouzes & Posner, 2002, page 84.
2. Kouzes & Posner, 2002, page 45.
3. Bill Gates, *Business Week*, March 22, 2005.
4. Bill Gates, speech to conference Microsoft Business Solutions Convergence 2005, San Diego, California, March 9, 2005.
5. Gary Hamel, 2000.

Chapter 7
1. Kouzes & Posner, 2002.
2. James M. Kouzes and Barry Z. Posner, The Leadership Challenge, Jossey Bass, 1987, page xi.
3. Kouzes & Posner, 2002, page 156.
4. Kouzes & Posner, 2002.
5. Kouzes & Posner, 2002, page 15.
6. Kouzes & Posner, 2002, page 17.
7. Kouzes & Posner, 2002, page 17.
8. Kouzes & Posner, 2002, page 17.
9. Kouzes & Posner, 2002, page 17.
10. Bernard Bass and & Bruce Avolio in Bernard Bass & Bruce Avolio, *Improving Organizational Effectiveness*, Sage Publications, Inc, 1994, page 3.
11. Bernard Bass and & Bruce Avolio, 1994, page 3.

Chapter 8
1. Sally Helgeson, *The Female Advantage*, Currency Doubleday, 1995, page 7.
2. Helgeson, 1995, page 7.
3. Joyce K. Fletcher & Katrin Kaufer, Shared Leadership in Craig L. Pearce & Jay A. Conger, *Shared Leadership*, Sage Publications, Inc, 2003, page 27.
4. Fletcher & Kaufer, 2003, page 27.

Chapter 9
1. Daniel Goleman, Emotional Intelligence, New York: Bantam Books, 1995.
2. Daniel Goleman, What Makes a Leader?, Harvard Business Review, Nov/Dec, 1998, page 93.
3. Goleman, 1998, page 94.
4. Goleman, 1998, page 99.

Chapter 11
1. Larry C. Spears, editor, *Reflections on Leadership*, John Wiley & Sons, 1995.
2. Spears, 1995, page 3.

Acknowledgements

I am indebted to the following for comments they made on specific parts of the book or who have debated leadership ideas with me in recent years:

Jean-Pierre Bal, Steve Kelly, Thomas Kent, Erwin Rausch Sjoerd Talsma and BH Tan.

Naturally, any remaining lack of clarity and errors are my responsibility.

Index

3M, 112, 120
anxiety, 4, 60, 62, 65, 75, 78, 80, 83, 87, 165–6, 168, 171, 175–6, 178
Apple, 15, 120
Avolio, Bruce, 181

Ballmer, Steve, 94
Barnard, Christiaan, 95
Bass, Bernard, 117, 181
Bennis, Warren, 34, 180
born leaders, 51
bottom-up leadership, 2–3, 5–7, 15–16, 18, 22, 27, 40, 49, 96–9, 103, 116, 133, 140, 147, 149
Bower, Tom, 28, 44, 59, 61, 75, 87, 104, 179

career management, 96, 101–2
catalyst, 36, 43–4, 64–8, 75, 87–8
character, 10, 23, 58, 92, 107, 132–7, 141
charisma, 41, 48, 56–7, 147
Churchill, Winston, 51–2, 61
Citrin, James, 180
coach, 30–1, 36, 43–4, 64–6, 68, 73, 75, 87–8, 92–3, 96–7, 150, 158, 169
Collins, Jim, 43–4, 87–8, 93, 140, 169, 180
complexity, 2, 12, 42, 45, 49, 53, 83, 105, 121–2, 130, 140, 165, 174
content leadership, 25, 55–6, 65, 71, 94, 146
courage, 3–9, 13, 47–8, 50–1, 58, 89–91, 105–6, 123, 128, 147, 177

creativity, 3, 6, 8–10, 13, 44, 90–1, 138, 146, 149, 159, 165, 169, 170

emergent, 20, 149, 150–1, 156, 165
emotional intelligence, 2–3, 6, 10, 21, 23–5, 50, 58, 63, 70, 86, 92, 107, 113, 132, 137–41, 158, 177, 181
empowerment, 5, 28, 59, 73, 85–6, 101, 106, 116, 150–2, 167, 169
entrepreneurship, 97, 135, 138–9, 146–7, 152
executive development, 93, 95–6, 104

fear, 59, 79–81, 85, 90–1, 97, 168
Fletcher, Joyce, 130, 181
fostering leadership, 95–6, 98, 104, 123

Gandhi, Mahatma, 5–7, 15–17, 120
Gates, Bill, 70, 94, 120, 181
Godin, Seth, 22, 179
Goleman, Daniel, 23, 86, 137–9, 181
Greenleaf Robert, 160
Grove, Andy, 138

Hamel, Gary, 18, 49, 99, 179–81
Harvard Business Review, 32, 179, 181
Heifetz, Ronald, 67, 180
Helgeson, Sally, 127, 181
Hesse, Herman, 160
Hitler, Adolf 61, 134
Hussein, Saddam 134

influencing skills, 6, 8–9, 19, 41, 48, 50–1, 58, 85, 90, 98, 104, 106, 111–12, 127–8, 129, 131, 140, 159
informal leadership, 8, 17, 58, 61, 121
integrity, 2–3, 58, 63, 92, 111, 113, 132–3, 135, 136, 141, 177
investor, 34, 65–7, 75, 87

Kaufer, Katrin, 130, 181
Kelleher, Herb, 42
King, Martin Luther, 5–7, 15–17, 25, 34, 48, 53, 72, 85, 90, 120, 173
Kotter, John, 38–9, 40, 180
Kouzes, James, 9, 22, 92, 107, 109–17, 179, 181

Leadership Challenge, The, 9–10, 22, 92, 107, 109, 116, 179, 181
leadership development, 3, 13, 87, 89–93, 106, 159
leadership opportunities, 101–3, 128
level 5 leaders, 43, 129
Lewin, Roger, 180
Lincoln, 51
Ludwig, Arnold, 77–8, 180

Magretta, Joan, 34, 180
Mandela, Nelson, 5–7, 15–17, 173
mechanistic organizations, 150–3, 154
Microsoft, 15, 94, 120, 147, 181
military leadership, 140
myths of leadership, 8, 105

Nader, Ralph, 134
Napoleon, 51
Neff, Thomas, 180
Nicholson, Nigel, 78, 180

organic organization, 149, 151–3, 165

paternal leadership, 136, 175
paternalism, 4, 62, 79, 82, 84
Peters, Tom, 22, 32, 109
political leadership, 77, 126
Posner, Barry, 9, 22, 92, 107, 109–14, 116–17, 179, 181
postmodern, 11, 107, 165–72, 178

primitive leadership, 8, 76–7, 86, 106, 117, 140, 171, 178
process leadership, 25, 55–7, 68, 70–1, 74

Regine, Girute, 180
relationships, 2, 10, 24–5, 33, 81, 85, 104, 107, 119–22, 125–27, 129, 177

servant leadership, 11, 107, 145, 160–4
Sherman, Stafford, 180
Spears, Larry, 182
Stalin, 134
Steward, 65–6, 68, 87

Taylor, Frederick, 31–3, 35, 39
team leadership, 100
theory X, 7, 33, 39, 128
theory Y, 7, 8, 33, 39, 74, 128, 180
thought leadership, 8, 5, 7, 13, 15, 17, 18, 22–4, 27, 37, 40, 48–50, 53–55, 60–1, 92–3, 95, 98–9, 101, 105, 110–12, 114, 116–18, 120, 126, 129, 133, 135, 145, 149, 156–7, 159, 162–3, 170–1, 176
Tichy, Noel, 73
transactional analysis, 81
transformational leadership, 40, 117

vision, 5, 8, 11, 16, 26, 35, 57, 60, 69, 74, 88, 94–5, 110, 112–15, 126, 169, 175

Weill, Sandy, 42, 180
Welch, Jack, 32, 34, 52, 71–4, 76
Wells, John, 21, 23, 26, 30, 46–7, 64, 179
women as leader, 10, 119, 126

youthful rebelliousness, 3, 50, 149, 170
Yukl, Gary, 53, 180

Zaleznik, Abraham, 32–4, 39, 78, 170, 179–80